# Armies of the Scythians and Sarmatians 700 BC to AD 450

Gabriele Esposito is a military historian who works as a freelance author and researcher for some of the most important publishing houses in the military history sector. In particular, he is an expert specializing in uniformology: his interests and expertise range from the ancient civilizations to modern post-colonial conflicts. During recent years, he has conducted and published several researches on the military history of the Latin American countries, with special attention on the War of the Triple Alliance and the War of the Pacific. He is among the leading experts on the military history of the Italian Wars of Unification and the Spanish Carlist Wars. His books and essays are published on a regular basis by Osprey Publishing, Winged Hussar Publishing and Libreria Editrice Goriziana. He is also the author of numerous military history articles appearing in specialized magazines such as *Ancient Warfare Magazine*, *Medieval Warfare Magazine*, *The Armourer*, *History of War*, *Guerres et Histoire*, *Focus Storia* and *Focus Storia Wars*.

# Armies of the Scythians and Sarmatians 700 BC to AD 450

Weapons, Equipment and Tactics

Gabriele Esposito

Pen & Sword
MILITARY

First published in Great Britain in 2024 by
Pen & Sword Military
An imprint of
Pen & Sword Books Limited
Yorkshire – Philadelphia

Copyright © Gabriele Esposito 2024

ISBN 978 1 39904 735 7

The right of Gabriele Esposito to be identified as
Author of this Work has been asserted by him in accordance
with the Copyright, Designs and Patents Act 1988.

A CIP catalogue record for this book is
available from the British Library

All rights reserved. No part of this book may be reproduced or
transmitted in any form or by any means, electronic or mechanical
including photocopying, recording or by any information storage and
retrieval system, without permission from the Publisher in writing.

Typeset by Mac Style
Printed and bound in India by Replika Press Pvt. Ltd.

Pen & Sword Books Limited incorporates the imprints of After the Battle, Atlas, Archaeology, Aviation, Discovery, Family History, Fiction, History, Maritime, Military, Military Classics, Politics, Select, Transport, True Crime, Air World, Frontline Publishing, Leo Cooper, Remember When, Seaforth Publishing, The Praetorian Press, Wharncliffe Local History, Wharncliffe Transport, Wharncliffe True Crime and White Owl.

For a complete list of Pen & Sword titles please contact

PEN & SWORD BOOKS LIMITED
47 Church Street, Barnsley, South Yorkshire, S70 2AS, England
E-mail: enquiries@pen-and-sword.co.uk
Website: www.pen-and-sword.co.uk
or
PEN AND SWORD BOOKS
1950 Lawrence Rd, Havertown, PA 19083, USA
E-mail: uspen-and-sword@casematepublishers.com
Website: www.penandswordbooks.com

# Contents

| | | |
|---|---|---|
| *Acknowledgements* | | vi |
| *Introduction* | | vii |
| **Chapter 1** | The Early History of the Scythians | 1 |
| **Chapter 2** | The Golden Age of the Scythians | 16 |
| **Chapter 3** | The Scythians and the Greco-Persian Wars | 36 |
| **Chapter 4** | The Decline of the Scythians | 71 |
| **Chapter 5** | Military Organization and Equipment of the Scythians | 90 |
| **Chapter 6** | The Early History of the Sarmatians | 103 |
| **Chapter 7** | The Sarmatians and the Dacian Wars | 116 |
| **Chapter 8** | The Decline of the Sarmatians | 133 |
| **Chapter 9** | Military Organization and Equipment of the Sarmatians | 141 |
| *Bibliography* | | 146 |
| *The Re-enactors who Contributed to this Book* | | 147 |
| *Index* | | 151 |

# Acknowledgements

This book is dedicated to my magnificent parents, Maria Rosaria and Benedetto, for the immense love and fundamental support that they always give me. Thanks to their precious advice deriving from long experience, the present book has turned out much better than I could ever have hoped for. A very special thanks goes to Philip Sidnell, the commissioning editor of my books for Pen & Sword: his love for history and his passion for publishing are the key factors behind the success of our publications. Many thanks also to the production manager of this title, Matt Jones, for his excellent work and great enthusiasm. A special mention is due to Tony Walton, for the magnificent work of editing that he makes for all my books. A very special mention goes to the brilliant re-enactment groups that collaborated with their photographs to the creation of this book: without the incredible work of research of their members, the final result of this publication would have not been the same. As a result, I want to express my deep gratitude to the following living history associations: Scythian State from Ukraine, Amages Drachen from Germany, Ancient Thrace from Bulgaria and Historia Renascita from Romania. This book is dedicated to the memory of Sergey Meleshko, the leader of the group Scythian State, who left us a few months before the publication of the present work.

# Introduction

The main aim of this book is to present a detailed analysis of the military history, organization and equipment of two ancient peoples living on the steppes of Eurasia: the Scythians and the Sarmatians. They were part of the Indo-Europeans and originated in the heart of Central Asia, from where they migrated towards the vast plains of southern Russia and Ukraine. Like all the steppe peoples of Antiquity and of the Middle Ages, the Scythians and Sarmatians were described as 'masters of horses' by the sedentary peoples living around them. Being nomads who were constantly on the move, the Scythians and Sarmatians spent most of their lives on horses, which were a fundamental component of their civilizations. Life was very harsh for these nomadic peoples, who did not practice agriculture but had large amounts of cattle. To find the pastures needed to feed their cattle, they moved across the wild plains of the steppe following the course of the major rivers. All the Scythian and Sarmatian men were warriors, who travelled on horseback, their families following them on carts, which acted as their 'moving houses'. Scythian and Sarmatian society was quite simple and egalitarian, since all the free men had the right to bear arms and to fight in case of war. There was a powerful nobility made up of warlords and their personal retainers, but these did not enjoy particular privileges. The priests tasked with performing religious rites made up a separate component of Scythian and Sarmatian society, being the guardians of their people's traditions. Both the Scythians and the Sarmatians owned slaves, who could be foreigners captured during military incursions or individuals from the local communities of southern Russia/Ukraine that had been submitted by the steppe peoples during their migrations. Slave trading always remained an important economic activity of the Scythians and Sarmatians. It should be noted, however, that these two steppe peoples were extremely advanced from a cultural point of view. First of all, their women enjoyed a series of liberties that could not be found in any other society of the ancient world: they were permitted to live and fight as men and enjoyed the same rights. Indeed, the famous myth of the Amazons originated after the Greeks met the warrior women of the Scythians.

The Scythians and Sarmatians were the first peoples of history, together with the Cimmerians and the Massagetae, to deploy massive cavalry armies. These were totally different from the forces of their opponents from the Mediterranean world or from Mesopotamia, which mostly consisted of infantry. Riding sturdy horses and equipped with deadly composite bows, Scythian mounted archers faced – and on most occasions defeated – all the most important armies of Antiquity: Assyrians, Medes, Persians, Greeks and Macedonians. The Sarmatians, who were the direct heirs of the Scythians, were among the fiercest enemies of the Roman Empire for several centuries. They introduced to Europe the new troop type of the heavily armoured lancer, which was soon copied by the Romans. Both the Scythians and the Sarmatians have left us many burial sites containing massive amounts of weapons; as a result, over recent decades it has been possible to reconstruct how they were equipped for war and which tactics they employed on the battlefield. Judging from surviving pieces of military equipment, they had incredible metalworking capabilities and produced some of the finest weapons ever seen during Antiquity. Reconstructing the military history and organization of the Scythians and Sarmatians, however, is much more difficult since they did not leave any written sources. Consequently, what we know about them mostly derives from the works of great Greek and Roman authors. In this work we will detail the history of the Scythians and the Sarmatians from their early arrival in Europe to their final disappearance, along with the military organization and equipment of both peoples.

# Chapter 1

## The Early History of the Scythians

The historical origins of the Scythians are still a matter of debate among modern scholars, since we have no written primary sources produced by them detailing their early history. Two hypotheses have emerged during the past decades, which are based on different sources and evidence. The first, supported by most of the modern Russian academics, is based on what the great Greek historian Herodotus wrote about the origins of the Scythians. According to him, they were an Eastern Iranian-speaking group that settled in a geographical region known as Inner Asia, comprising the area between present-day Turkestan and Western Siberia. The second hypothesis, supported by several scholars of the Anglo-Saxon world, proposes that the Scythians emerged as a new civilization from groups belonging to a local culture that existed along the Black Sea coast (the so-called Srubna Culture). What we know for sure is that the Black Sea region, roughly corresponding to modern southern Ukraine, became the homeland of the Scythians from 700 BC. Herodotus and his modern followers thought that the Scythians migrated to the Black Sea region from Inner Asia; but according to the second hypothesis supported by the Anglo-Saxon scholars, the Scythians originated in the Black Sea region as a result of the area's cultural evolution. Recent genetic studies have shown that the Scythians were strongly linked to the peoples of Inner Asia and had many elements in common with them. As a result, it is highly probable that Herodotus' reconstruction of the early history of the Scythians was correct. During the early Iron Age, several peoples living in Inner Asia migrated across the steppes to reach southern Russia and Ukraine. These mass migrations of peoples remained a distinctive element of Inner Asia during most of Antiquity and had enormous consequences for the history of European civilization. Broadly speaking, the migratory movements were usually caused by the emergence of new regional powers in the steppes of Inner Asia. When a new military power emerged – this could consist of a single people or a confederation of peoples – it started to expand its own territories by attacking the other steppe peoples living on its borders. If defeated in battle, the communities attacked by the emerging power had no choice but to migrate westwards in search of new lands to live upon. Moving westwards meant abandoning the heartland of the Asian steppes to enter Europe, where other civilizations had already developed themselves in a significant way.

Scythian heavy cavalryman. (*Photo and copyright by Scythian State*)

Around 800 BC, the Scythians were attacked in their homeland of Inner Asia by another steppe people of nomads, the Massagetae. The latter came to control a sizeable portion of the territory located east of the Caspian Sea and were much more numerous than the Scythians. After conquering the Scythian homeland in Inner Asia, they became an important military power and started to represent a menace for the advanced civilizations of ancient Iran. After Cyrus the Great formed the Achaemenid Empire by uniting the Persians and the Medes who both lived in Iran, the Massagetae became the main enemies of the Achaemenid monarch. Initially,

Scythian helmet. (*Photo and copyright by Scythian State*)

Cyrus tried to avoid a direct confrontation with them, knowing their great combat capabilities; he offered a peace treaty to them and proposed to marry the queen of the Massagetae. Cyrus' offers, however, were turned down by the Massagetae, who started to attack the north-eastern territories of the Achaemenid Empire. Cyrus the Great responded by launching an invasion of Massagetae lands around 530 BC, advancing towards the Jaxartes River at the head of a large army. The Massagetae employed elusive military tactics, exactly like the Scythians and the other steppe peoples of the time; so it was very difficult for the Persians of Cyrus to intercept them and force them to give battle. Hoping to trick his enemies, Cyrus left behind a small portion of his invading army in an isolated position, whereupon the Massagetae, seeing an opportunity to obtain a decisive victory, attacked the Persian contingent. Before these could be destroyed, however, Cyrus arrived on the battlefield at the head of the rest of his army and soundly defeated the Massagetae. The Massagetae did not surrender after this setback, continuing to provoke the Persian invading force. After assembling another massive army, they challenged Cyrus the Great on the open field. During the ensuing battle, which was one of the largest ever fought on the Eurasian steppes, the Persians were defeated due to the numerical superiority of their enemy. According to Herodotus' description of this clash, Cyrus was killed in combat by the Massagetae, although the veracity of this is uncertain. What is known for sure is that the Massagetae obtained a great military success that secured their independence from the Achaemenid Empire for decades to come. The great military resources of the Massagetae, meanwhile, overwhelmed the Scythians, who were forced to abandon Inner Asia due to their foe's expansionist pressure. The Scythians crossed much of southern Russia before entering Ukraine, a region of Europe where there were all the necessary conditions for creating a new homeland. Southern Ukraine had vast plains with abundant pasture for the horses and was rich in water, making it would a perfect choice for a nomadic people like the Scythians who considered horses their most important properties.

When the Scythians arrived in southern Ukraine, however, the region was already inhabited by another steppe people: the Cimmerians. These originated in Inner Asia, just like the Scythians, and had migrated to the Pontic Steppe of southern Ukraine long before the Scythians; they are mentioned in Homer's *Odyssey*, meaning they already had contact with the Greek world from the ninth century BC onwards. The Ukrainian homeland of the Cimmerians extended from the high mountains of the Caucasus to the coastline of Crimea. According to Herodotus, the Cimmerians had submitted the original local inhabitants of southern Ukraine and absorbed them into their own people, but within Cimmerian society there was a clear division between the so-called 'royal race' descended from the original Cimmerians and the inferior 'common race' descended from the native inhabitants of pre-Cimmerian southern Ukraine. When the Scythians invaded the Pontic Steppe, numerous great battles took place between the newcomers and the Cimmerians, but due to the lack of written sources we know practically nothing of this conflict, which probably lasted for several decades. What we know for sure, however, is that the Scythians prevailed and expelled the Cimmerians from southern Ukraine. Most of the ancient wars fought among nomadic peoples of the steppes were won by the migrating tribes and not by those defending their home territories, mostly due to the fact that the migrating communities were more numerous than the settled ones and needed to conquer a new homeland to survive. After having been defeated by the Scythians, the Cimmerians moved southwards across the Caucasus. They tried to stop in modern Georgia, in a region that was known as Colchis during Antiquity, but here they were attacked again by the Scythians, who were pursuing them with the objective of obtaining complete control over the Caucasus. The Cimmerians were forced to move again and eventually settled in the region of Transcaucasia, roughly corresponding to modern Azerbaijan and north-eastern Turkey. Transcaucasia, in its western portion, was dominated by the Kingdom of Urartu, which was centred around Lake Van and was inhabited by a confederation of Armenian mountain tribes that had gradually formed a unified realm. Before the arrival of the Cimmerians, the Kingdom of Urartu was a significant regional power of Anatolia (modern Turkey) and one of the Assyrian Empire's fiercest enemies. Around 720 BC, according to some surviving primary sources, the Assyrians were informed that the Kingdom of Urartu had been attacked and defeated by some newcomers from the steppes. These were the Cimmerians, who were able to conquer the whole territory of Urartu quite easily due to their military superiority; the Armenian mountaineers were excellent infantrymen but had never faced in battle a steppe people like the Cimmerians, who deployed both mounted archers and heavily armoured cavalry. After overrunning Urartu, the Cimmerians continued their advance towards northern Mesopotamia and invested the northern borders of the Assyrian Empire. Here, in 705 BC, they fought a massive battle against the Assyrians but were defeated, although during this clash the Assyrian monarch, Sargon II, was killed.

After these events, most of the Cimmerians migrated into eastern Anatolia in order to avoid further confrontations with the Assyrians, but some groups remained in Transcaucasia where they continued to fight against the Assyrian Empire employing hit-and-run tactics. The Cimmerians of Anatolia remained a significant military power after their defeat of 705 BC and continued to fight against the Assyrians for several decades. Around 675 BC, they conquered the Kingdom of Phrygia in Anatolia, which was inhabited by a people of Thracian stock. During

Scythian vambrace (forearm guard) (*Photo and copyright by Scythian State*)

the following decades they continued their territorial expansion by conquering various Anatolian regions: Cappadocia, Bithynia, Paphlagonia and the Troad (thus reaching the Mediterranean). The Cimmerians also attacked the Kingdom of Lydia, at that time the dominant regional power of Anatolia. The Lydian monarch Gyges, however, defeated them in 665 BC, thereby saving the independence of his realm. During the period from 705–660 BC, the Cimmerians fought several wars against the Assyrian Empire and obtained many victories, the Assyrian army experiencing serious tactical difficulties in fighting the Cimmerians. The Assyrians had highly

Scythian heavy cavalryman. (*Photo and copyright by Scythian State*)

disciplined and well-equipped heavy infantry, but their cavalry were not fast-moving like those of the Cimmerians. In addition, most of the Cimmerian horsemen were equipped with the deadly composite bow of the steppes, while the Assyrian missile troops employed normal bows made entirely of wood. The frequent wars fought with the Cimmerians obliged the Assyrians to re-equip part of their forces in the Cimmerian style. This is confirmed by some surviving primary sources, according to which the portion of Assyrian troops tasked with fighting against the Cimmerians in the north was known as the Cimmerian Contingent, which employed the same fighting methods as their nomadic opponents. In 644 BC, taking advantage of the Assyrians' political and military difficulties, the Cimmerians invaded Lydia and finally captured it after killing King Gyges. After taking the Lydian capital of Sardis, the Cimmerians attacked the Greek colonies located on the Anatolian coastline. While they did not permanently occupy these, they conducted several violent raids that led to the destruction of the Temple of Artemis in Ephesus. Around 640 BC, the Cimmerians conquered Cilicia but could not prevent the resurgence of the Kingdom of Lydia. In 637 BC, the Cimmerians attacked and defeated the Lydians again, which persuaded the Assyrians to form an anti-Cimmerian alliance with the Scythians with the objective of stabilizing the north-western frontier of their empire. A massive Scythian army, led by King Madyes, then entered Anatolia and defeated the Cimmerians on behalf of the Assyrians. After having been crushed by their worst enemies, the Cimmerians ceased to represent a menace for the stability of the Assyrian Empire and lost their role as an Anatolian military power. What remained of the Cimmerian presence in Anatolia was ended by the Kingdom of Lydia, which defeated the last Cimmerian communities. By 600 BC, the Cimmerians had completely disappeared as a distinct people, their surviving elements having been absorbed into the local Anatolian communities.

After expelling the Cimmerians from southern Ukraine, the Scythians settled in the region and started to dominate the Pontic Steppe. Being numerous and warlike, they expanded westwards, where they came into contact with another nomadic people already settled in southern Ukraine: the Agathyrsi. These had been the first people of the steppes to colonize the Ukrainian plains and had established their new European homeland around the Sea of Azov. The Scythians pushed the Agathyrsi westwards and defeated them on several occasions, as a result of which the Agathyrsi were forced to settle in the territories of present-day Moldavia and Transylvania (northern Romania). Living over a vast region located north of the Danube and east of the Carpathian Mountains, the Agathyrsi established positive relations with the local peoples of Thracian stock. The first important king of the Scythians about whom we have some information was Bartatua, who created good

Scythian waistbelt covered with scales. (*Photos and copyright by Scythian State*)

diplomatic relations with the Assyrians and – in 672 BC – married a daughter of the Assyrian Emperor Esarhaddon. Bartatua was succeeded by his son Madyes, who expanded Scythian territories by conducting a series of military campaigns. In 653 BC, Madyes attacked the Medes in order to help his Assyrian allies, who were coming under increasing Mede pressure.

The Medes were a confederation of tribes that occupied a good portion of north-western Iran, living on a harsh mountain territory that was centred on Ecbatana. For a long time they played no significant role in the politics of the Ancient Middle

East, since they were vassals of the Assyrians. From 626 BC, however, the Assyrian Empire started to be ravaged by a series of civil wars that caused great political instability; the Medes took advantage of this new situation, like other communities that had been vassals of the Assyrians, and thereby regained most of their original autonomy. The great difficulties experienced by the Assyrian Empire were exploited to the full by the powerful city of Babylon, the largest and richest urban centre of the Ancient Middle East. The Babylonians formed a military alliance with the Medes and launched a series of major offensives against the Assyrians during the years 616–609 BC. These led to the final and definitive collapse of the Assyrian Empire, an event that changed the history of the Ancient Middle East forever. The Medes, who had occupied the Assyrian capital of Nineveh in 612 BC with the help of some Scythian contingents, gained many advantages from the rapid fall of the Assyrian Empire: they transformed their kingdom into an important regional power that dominated over a vast portion of Iran and started to play a significant role in the political scene of Mesopotamia. Following the collapse of the Assyrian Empire, a new system of power emerged in the Ancient Middle East, based on the co-existence of four powers that had all contributed – in different ways – to the fall of the Assyrians: Babylon, the Kingdom of Media, the Kingdom of Lydia and Egypt. During this historical phase, the Persians, who inhabited those areas of Iran that were not under the Medes' direct control, were semi-autonomous vassals of the Kingdom of Media. In 553 BC, the leader of the Persians, the future Cyrus the Great, revolted against Astyages of Media. After three years of campaigning, in 550 BC, a decisive battle took place between the Persians and the Medes, who had previously been allies in their struggle against the Assyrians. Cyrus and his Persians emerged victorious, capturing Astyages, who was abandoned by most of his nobles. Following these important events, Cyrus the Great unified the Persians and the Medes into a single political entity and founded the new Achaemenid Empire. The Medes were not humiliated by the victors, since they retained a prominent position in the new multinational empire of Cyrus and were second only to the Persians in terms of military prestige. Many of the most prominent generals and provincial governors of the Achaemenid Empire were Medes, while Ecbatana, the most important city of the Medes, became one of the Achaemenid Empire's capitals.

The temporary ascendancy of the Medes had negative consequences for the Scythians, who had been loyal allies of the Assyrian Empire for several decades. As referred to above, in 653 BC the Scythians mounted an invasion of Media that had some success, the nomadic warriors defeating the Medes in battle and – according to some ancient sources – even killing their king. For several years, the Scythians from the Caucasus were able to exert a strong influence over Media, which became one

Back view of a Scythian heavy cavalryman. (*Photo and copyright by Scythian State*)

Scythian corselet of scale armour. (*Photo and copyright by Scythian State*)

of their vassals. This, however, did not last long due to the many political changes that took place during the following years and which led to the ascendancy of the Persians. The brief golden age of the Scythians in the Middle East saw them controlling a good portion of Anatolia after having freed it from the Cimmerians. Scythian territories, however, were too extensive to be effectively controlled by a single monarch. The homeland of the Scythians, located north of the Caucasus in southern Ukraine, was too far from Anatolia and from Media, and the Scythians did not have seafaring capabilities and thus could not cross the Black Sea from Crimea to northern Anatolia in order to transport reinforcements or supplies. As a result of this situation, the Medes were able to regain most of their military power soon after having been defeated by the Scythians. In 625 BC, the Medes obtained a clear victory over the Scythians and freed themselves from their political control. With the fall of the Assyrian Empire, the Scythians lost their most important ally in Mesopotamia. However, they tried to take advantage of the new power vacuum, just like all the other peoples whose expansionist ambitions had previously been hampered by the Assyrians.

Between 623 and 616 BC, the Scythians launched a series of long-range incursions across the Middle East, raiding and pillaging with incredible violence. The nomadic warriors, who had never seen the riches of the Mesopotamian civilizations before, were greatly attracted by the massive amounts of gold that could be found in the towns and cities they raided. None of the four powers that had emerged after the fall of the Assyrian Empire – Babylon, the Kingdom of Media, Kingdom of Lidya and Egypt – had the military resources to stop the Scythian incursions. The cavalry armies of the steppe nomads moved rapidly from one region to another and could not be intercepted by the slow infantry forces of their opponents. The Scythians seemed unstoppable, terrorizing a vast portion of Mesopotamia before moving towards Palestine and Egypt, raiding every settlement they encountered along the way. Fearing that his realm could be conquered by the nomad warriors, the Egyptian Pharaoh Psamtik I met with Scythian leaders and offered favourable peace terms. The Egyptians paid a large sum of money to the Scythians and gave them many rich gifts in order to prevent the pillaging of their homeland. Around 615 BC, however, the incursions conducted across the Middle East by the Scythians ceased when the Medes strongly attacked the Scythian territories in Anatolia. The ensuing conflict fought between the Medes and Scythians lasted for a couple of decades, with the Medes gradually gaining the upper hand. By 590 BC, the Medes had conquered the Anatolian possessions of the Scythians, who were obliged to go back north of the Caucasus. The first phase of Scythian expansionism was over and they would never again play an important role in the politics of the Middle East. Most of the Scythian groups that had settled south of the Caucasus went back to the Pontic Steppe, from where they started to look towards the northern Balkans for further territorial expansion. A few Scythian communities remained in the Middle East, but these were quite isolated and were all progressively absorbed by the Medes.

The ascendancy of Cyrus the Great and his Persians armies changed the existing political situation in the Middle East in a dramatic way. Soon after submitting the Medes, the Achaemenid monarch turned his attention towards the rich city of Babylon, which controlled a good portion of Mesopotamia but had inferior military resources compared with the Achaemenid Empire. In 539 BC, the joint forces of the

Scythian shield. (*Photo and copyright by Scythian State*)

Persians and Medes attacked Babylon and besieged it. The city fell after a short siege, having been racked by internal political divisions. With the conquest of Babylon, the Achaemenid Empire became the dominant military power of the Middle East, also annexing that portion of Assyria that had previously been controlled by Babylon.

Scythian sword. (*Photo and copyright by Scythian State*)

During 547 and 546 BC, before investing Babylon, the Persians and Medes of Cyrus the Great had conquered the Kingdom of Lydia, as a result of which, by 539 BC, the Achaemenid Empire included Anatolia. Of the four states that had benefited from the fall of the Assyrians, only Egypt remained independent, but within a few decades the Egyptians would also be defeated and conquered by the Achaemenid Empire. In this new world dominated by the Persians, although the Scythians no longer had any opportunities for expansion or raiding in the Middle East, they could find new lands to target in the Balkans.

# Chapter 2

# The Golden Age of the Scythians

The historical period lasting from 1100–800/700 BC was a particularly turbulent one for the southern Balkans, as with the end of the Bronze Age the great civilization of the Myceneans – who had long dominated over Greece – collapsed. The new historical period that started in 1100 BC is commonly known as the Greek Dark Ages or Greek Middle Ages, comprising a difficult phase of transition between the Mycenean civilization and the new Greek Classical one. These few centuries were characterized by a series of deep changes that affected many aspects of Greek society, including artistically and militarily. The Greek Dark Ages are also known as the Geometric Period because of the artistic decorations that became popular during that period, or as the Homeric Age since it was during this time that the famous Homeric poems were composed. These poems still contained many elements deriving from the Mycenean period, albeit mixed with some new ones established by the Dorian communities that invaded Greece at the beginning of the Greek Middle Ages. Mycenean society had been dominated by the figure of the *wanax*, or king, for centuries: the powerful aristocrat and warlord could count on the support of a personal retinue formed by many professional warriors. Each *wanax* controlled his realm from fortified palaces and citadels that were protected by gigantic cyclopic walls. With the Doric invasions, such settlements entered a rapid process of decay, the walled citadels and monumental palaces built by the Myceneans being abandoned and replaced by new cities that gradually developed from the small villages created by the newcomers. There is no doubt that this era of Greek history had some 'dark' features, but it would be a mistake to perceive it as a totally negative period of transformation. It was during the Greek Dark Ages, for example, that most of Greek Classical civilization's main features were shaped and firmly established. The complex political and military organization of the Myceneans disappeared, together with any form of centralized authority. The famous Mycenean Linear-B writing system was also abandoned, being replaced by a new Phoenician alphabet that gave birth to all the following alphabets in European and Mediterranean history. These material and cultural changes were extremely significant, causing a revolution in all the fields of human knowledge. By the beginning of the eighth century BC, a new and very positive age began in the history of Greece: economy and commerce

Scythian heavy cavalryman. (*Photo and copyright by Scythian State*)

started to flourish thanks to the period of stability that followed the end of the foreign invasions, the population began to grow very rapidly and this gave great impulse to a process of colonization by the Greeks.

With the end of the so-called Dark Ages, the population of mainland Greece started to grow at an impressive rate, and all the newly-founded *poleis* (independent cities/states) had to introduce measures to control the demography of their communities. Greece was still a poor country at the time and its territory was mostly

Scythian greaves. (*Photo and copyright by Scythian State*)

covered with mountains, so Greek cities could not practice agriculture on a large scale and were forced to resettle a major portion of their citizens outside the borders of mainland Greece. During the eighth and seventh centuries BC, many thousands of Greek colonists departed their mother cities in search of new lands to found their own *poleis*. These great migratory movements of the Greeks were directed towards the western Mediterranean, where they created many flourishing colonies in southern Italy, but also towards the coastline of the Black Sea that extended from Thrace in the west to the Caucasus in the east. The Ukrainian coastline of the Black Sea, including Crimea, had been settled by the Scythians just a few decades before, and thus it was on the shores of the Black Sea that the Greeks met the Scythians for the first time. The coastline of Thrace, extending from the Chalcidian Peninsula to the delta of the Danube, was the first target of the Greek colonists during their expansion in the east. When it was known that the hills inhabited by the Thracians were rich in precious metals such as gold or silver, Greek penetration into Thrace increased rapidly. The *poleis* of mainland Greece were in constant search of new natural resources in order to sustain the great commercial expansion of their communities: by founding new colonies in the east, they resolved the problem of over-population and also acquired control over strategic natural resources that were located in foreign lands. Before building new settlements, however, the Greeks had to fight the local Thracian tribes, who had no intention of welcoming the foreigners to their lands. During their early attempts to colonize the Thracian coastline, the Greeks experienced many difficulties, as the local population was a warlike one and the whole region was still in a 'wild' state by Greek standards of the time. Thrace, however, was a land of opportunities and the Greeks continued their attempts at colonization. During this early period, which lasted until the outbreak of the Persian Wars in the fifth century BC, the Greeks founded several new settlements along the coastline of southern Thrace. In particular, they penetrated into the strategic Chersonese Peninsula, a region that is part of Europe geographically but makes up the western side of the Dardanelles Straits. Consequently, the Greeks tried to obtain control over this peninsula, which was also known as the Thracian Chersonese. The rich commercial outposts established by the Greeks on the southern coast of Thrace soon transformed themselves into thriving cities, whose relations with the Thracians were complicated. After decades of minor warfare and frequent skirmishes, it became clear to the Thracian tribes that the Greek colonies could not be destroyed by them. The cities were well defended by thick walls and the Thracians were not able to conduct siege operations. During the following centuries, these centres would play an important historical role by connecting Greek culture with that of the Thracians.

The Greeks, starting from the seventh century BC, began founding several colonies on the Crimean coastline of the Black Sea. These small centres, initially created just to act as commercial outposts, soon transformed themselves into large and rich cities that controlled the trade routes of the northern Black Sea. The Greek colonies of Crimea, in particular, became fundamental in the development of strong commercial relations between the Scythians and the Greek world. Thanks to the massive exportation of wheat and grain, the Greek colonies of Crimea started to flourish and became increasingly important politically. Around 480 BC, probably to improve their military defence against the potential menace represented by the Scythians, the various Greek colonies of Crimea united themselves into a single political entity and formed a kingdom or confederation of cities. In 438 BC, the legitimate royal house of this realm was removed by a usurper named Spartocus, who soon initiated his own dynasty. The Spartocid royal house was able to expand its dominions by conquering new territories in southern Ukraine and submitting various Scythian groups. The expansionism of the Spartocids was halted in 310 BC by the outbreak of a civil war, which also caused some troubles for the flourishing economy of the kingdom. Initially, the military organization of the Greek colonies founded in Crimea was exactly the same as the cities in mainland Greece: each colony had its own small army of citizen-soldiers, who fought as hoplites. With the progression of time, as the Greek colonies became increasingly rich, the use of citizen-soldiers decreased considerably. Thanks to the vast amounts of money obtained from trade, the Greek colonists were able to raise substantial contingents of mercenaries. The Scythians were readily available for service as allies/subjects of the Greek colonies and could provide extremely large numbers of fighters. Since the beginning of the Greek colonization of the Ukrainian coastline, the relations established by the newcomers with the Scythians were quite positive, the Scythians understanding that the Greeks had no intention of conquering their lands but just wanted to build coastal centres devoted to commerce.

The Greek merchants were greatly interested in trading with the Scythians, since southern Ukraine produced large amounts of grain (badly needed in Greece) and was rich in natural resources like gold or silver. The Scythians, meanwhile, wanted to purchase luxury goods from the Greek merchants, such as wine, oil, vases, clothing and jewels. The Greek presence on the Ukrainian coastline did not represent a threat to the Scythians, who maintained peaceful relations with the Greeks for centuries. Small wars did occasionally take place between a Greek colony and a Scythian community, but these never lasted long and resulted in few casualties on both sides. The Greeks were too few to venture into the interior areas of Ukraine, and the Scythians were not capable of conducting the besieging operations needed to conquer a Greek colony. As a result, although the Greeks sometimes perceived the Scythians as a potential menace, in practice they never ran the risk of being expelled from their flourishing coastal cities. The first Greek city to be founded in Crimea was Panticapaeum, a colony of Miletus that was established during the late seventh century BC. Miletus, like the other Greek coastal cities of Anatolia (known as

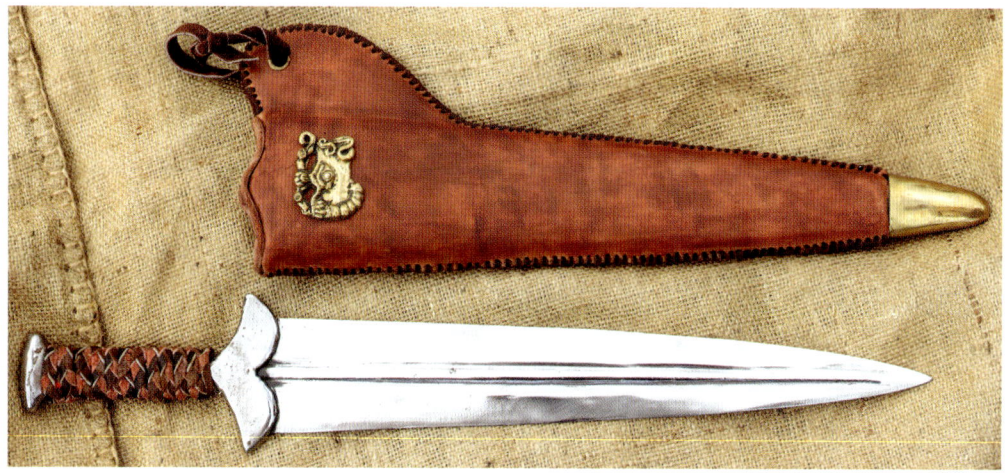

Scythian dagger. (*Photo and copyright by Scythian State*)

Scythian axe. (*Photo and copyright by Scythian State*)

Asia Minor by the Greeks), played a prominent role in the colonization of southern Ukraine's coastline. Panticapaeum soon became an important trading centre, mostly due to its geographical location on what later became known as Mount Mithridar, where the modern city of Kerch is now situated. The Greek colonists from Miletus imported large quantities of articles produced in their motherland and sold these to the Scythian nobility, importing pottery, terracotta goods and fine metal objects that were produced in various workshops around mainland Greece. At the same time, the Greeks of Crimea organized their own locally based production of vases, in order to have products of inferior quality but for reduced prices that could be sold to the Scythians of lower social status. Over time, many other Greek colonies were established on the coastline of southern Ukraine, where they prospered economically despite their small size. Colonies that were created by those originating from Miletus included Theodosia, Kimmerikon, Tyritake and Myrmekion. Theodosia became the most important Greek centre in Crimea for the export of wheat, which was produced in great quantities in southern Ukraine. Kimmerikon probably derived its name from the fact that it was founded on a previous settlement that had been inhabited by the Cimmerians. It was the main military stronghold of the Greeks in Crimea, since it was located on the western slope of Mount Opuk and was very difficult to besiege. Tyritake specialized in the production of crafts and in viticulture, but never became a large centre. Fishing eventually became another important component of the Greek colonies' economy, together with the production of wine.

The success of the early colonies convinced many more Greeks to leave their homeland for the distant area of the Black Sea, which was considered to be at the end of the world by most contemporary historians. The Greeks had no idea of what existed in the interior areas of Ukraine, but were sure that by being near to the sea they could receive all the necessary supplies in case of need. New urban centres were gradually erected on the coastline of Crimea; some of these, like Myrmekion, were

Scythian whip. (*Photo and copyright by Scythian State*)

not colonies but completely independent cities. These, like the colonies, prospered quite rapidly, to the point that they could protect themselves with towered walls and mint their own coinage. Around 570 BC, some colonists hailing from the city of Samos, the main rival of Miletus, founded their own city in Crimea: Nymphaion. This city assumed control over cereal trade and soon became a loyal ally of Athens, which needed increasingly large amounts of grain to feed its expanding population, and these could be imported only from Sicily or Ukraine. The Greek cities located

Scythian dagger. (*Photo and copyright by Scythian State*)

on the northern coastline of Anatolia were also particularly active in the colonization of southern Crimea. Some colonists from Heraclea Pontica, for example, founded the important sea port of Chersonesos (located very near to modern Sevastopol). In Crimea, the Greeks co-existed not only with the Scythians, but also with another mysterious people known as the Tauri. Very little is known about the Tauri, apart from that they inhabited the mountainous area located between the steppe of southern Ukraine and the coastline of Crimea. During Antiquity, this area was commonly known as Taurica. According to Herodotus, the Tauri were not part of the Scythians since, instead being the last heirs of the communities that had populated southern Ukraine before the arrival of the Cimmerians. According to Strabo, however, the Tauri were a sub-group of the Scythians. It is highly probable that both Herodotus and Strabo were right, with the Tauri being the native inhabitants of Crimea but gradually intermixing with the Scythians to the point of becoming undistinguishable from them. Some Greek authors, in fact, called the Tauri the Tauroscythians. From a cultural point of view, especially before establishing stable relations with the Greeks, the Tauri were a quite primitive people: they were, for example, famous for their custom of human sacrifice, which was considered an absolutely barbarian practice by the Greeks. Compared with the Scythians, the Tauri posed much more of a threat for the Greeks, establishing a military base at Symbolon (modern Balaklava) from which they launched raids and incursions against the Greek commercial outposts. The Tauri were also capable of navigating along the coast, which enabled them to engage in piracy, their main target being the Greek merchant ships exporting and importing valuable goods from Crimea. The Greeks colonized all the shores of the Black Sea: Thrace in the west, Ukraine in the north, Anatolia (Pontus) in the south and Colchis in the east. Colchis, roughly corresponding to present-day Georgia, was inhabited by several warlike tribes which, like the Tauri of Crimea, co-existed with the Scythians but were never completely submitted by them. The Colchians retained their autonomy because they populated the coastal areas of the western Caucasus, while the Scythians controlled the interior of the region. The Colchians traded with the Greeks but always limited the establishment of permanent Greek colonies on their home territory, being extremely warlike and quite primitive according to contemporary Greek standards. Colchis was a land of barbarians and mysteries for the Greeks, who did not have a precise knowledge of the interior expanses of the Caucasus. The famous Greek hero Jason and his Argonauts, in their quest for the Golden Fleece, had to reach Colchis to find their prize, fighting against the Colchians and various mysterious creatures before returning home victorious.

As we have seen, the western coast of Asia Minor had been progressively colonized by the Greeks, who created several new *poleis* in the region. These were assembled into two large communities, those of Aeolia and Ionia. Until 546 BC, the Greek cities of Asia Minor could flourish without problems and establish new colonies in Crimea, since they were not menaced by any bordering country, the internal part of Anatolia being controlled by the Kingdom of Lydia which had quite positive relations with the Greeks. Since 560 BC, Lydia had been ruled by King Croesus, who was one of the richest monarchs of his time. At the beginning of his reign, Croesus reasserted Lydia's formal dominance over Aeolia and Ionia, but the Greeks of Asia Minor were fully independent in practice and only had to pay a yearly tribute in gold to the Lydian king. The Kingdom of Lydia, with the city of Sardes as its capital, was one of the most powerful of the ancient world, but in 547 BC it started to be directly menaced by a new power appearing on the horizon: the Persian Empire. Ruled by the new Achaemenid dynasty founded by Cyrus the Great, the Persians had conquered most of the Middle East in a series of brilliant and rapid military campaigns. Anatolia was the next target of the Persians, who had an immense multi-ethnic army mostly made up of light troops. Croesus did not wait for the Persian invasion, but instead decided to attack first in 547 BC, his chances of success being boosted by alliances with Sparta, the Babylonian Empire and Egypt. After some inconclusive clashes fought in central Anatolia, the decisive battle took place in 546 BC at Thymbra, where Croesus was soundly defeated and retreated to his capital of Sardes, which was soon besieged and captured by the advancing Persians. The defeated king was seized and his realm was absorbed into the Persian Empire. A few years later, in 539 BC, Cyrus also conquered Babylon and thus completed the conquest of the Middle East. The Greeks of Aeolia and Ionia were now bordering a gigantic empire, which had no intention of preserving their previous privileges and liberties enjoyed under Croesus.

Indeed, Cyrus the Great soon organized an expedition against the Greek cities of Asia Minor, led by his Median general Harpagus. The Persians were able to subdue the *poleis* of western Anatolia after a brief campaign, but the Greeks were determined to keep up the fight. They proved to be very difficult to rule for the Persians, refusing to pay taxes and always being ready to rise up in open revolt. In most areas of his growing empire, like in Lydia, Cyrus the Great had formed an alliance with the various local aristocracies after defeating them, but such political manoeuvring proved impossible with the Greek cities of Asia Minor, where most of the citizens

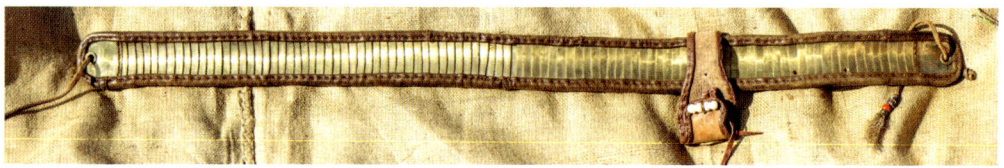

Scythian waistbelt covered with scales. (*Photo and copyright by Scythian State*)

Scythian quiver with arrows. (*Photo and copyright by Scythian State*)

had more or less the same rights and social position. For the first time, the Persians were dealing with a people made up of free individuals and not of subjects used to serving under a supreme monarch. The Achaemenids sponsored the ascendancy of tyrants in several *poleis*, but this was not enough to secure their control over Asia

Minor, most of the tyrants being soon killed or expelled by popular revolts. Most of the Greeks from Asia were sure that their compatriots from the mainland would help them against the foreign invader, as by the beginning of the fifth century BC western Anatolia was widely considered an organic part of the Greek world. The Persians, well aware of this, had plans to continue their expansion towards Greece in the future, and thus tried to form a network of alliances with cities of mainland Greece. While these events happened in the Aegean, the Persians continued to expand in other areas of the Mediterranean. After the death of Cyrus the Great, they conquered Egypt, which was of great military importance because absorbing the Egyptians among their subjects meant the Achaemenids were able to count on large contingents of sailors and naval infantry. The Persians were used to the traditional land-based warfare of Iran and had no experience of naval campaigns, but with the conquest of the Phoenicians and then the Egyptians they were able to build an impressive fleet with which they could start planning an attack against Greece.

By 520 BC, the military expansion of the Persians had pushed their empire to the borders of the Scythian territories in the Caucasus. The Persians, well aware of the great military capabilities of the Scythians, considered them as dangerous potential enemies. The Achaemenid monarchs had plans to transform the Black Sea into a Persian lake and were determined to take control over the trade networks established by the Greeks of Asia Minor. To do this, they had no alternative but to invade the Scythian lands of southern Ukraine; once in this region, the Persians would have been able to occupy Crimea and gain access to all the important resources of the territory. The Achaemenid Empire was by now ruled by the ambitious Darius I, who was determined to expand his lands by moving westwards. Around 515 BC, he sent a small naval expedition, consisting of thirty warships commanded by the satrap (governor) of Cappadocia, to the northern shore of the Black Sea. The Persians explored the area and conducted a series of devastating raids, which resulted in the capture of many Scythians, who were transported to Persia as slaves. The positive results achieved by this small-scale naval expedition convinced Darius that an invasion of Ukraine was possible. Instead of attacking Scythian lands from the east, by moving north of the Caucasus Mountains, the Persians decided to cross the Black Sea at the Bosphorus Straits by building a massive bridge of boats. They did so for two main reasons: first, crossing the Caucasus with a large army was an impossible task at the time; and second, the construction of a bridge of boats at the Bosphorus would shock the Greeks and establish a strategic infrastructure that would be vital for a future invasion of Greece. To reach Scythian lands, which were located north of the Danube River, the Persians were obliged to cross the southern portion of the eastern Balkans that was inhabited by the Thracians.

Scythian heavy cavalryman. (*Photo and copyright by Scythian State*)

Scythian heavy cavalryman wearing a modified version of the Greek Chalcidian helmet. (*Photo and copyright by Amages Drachen*)

Since the beginning of the eighth century BC, the Thracians had been one of the most flourishing peoples of Europe. They occupied a vast area of the Balkans located south of the Danube and had established a firm control over a significant part of Anatolia, consisting of the regions of Phrygia and Bithynia, which became Asian kingdoms but whose populations never lost their original Thracian culture. However, the Thracians of Europe did not develop any long-lasting form of unified kingdom. They were divided into more than forty tribes, which were constantly at war against each other. Indeed, Thracian society was an extremely violent one, in which warfare was considered as one of the most important elements in a man's life. From an economic point of view, the Thracians practiced animal breeding much more than agriculture, the great majority of them being shepherds and making a living from the products obtained from their sheep and goats. Inter-tribal skirmishes and raids were usually sparked by disputes between shepherds over control of their pastures. The majority of the Thracians did not live in permanent settlements, instead following their herds during most of the year. Consequently, until the arrival of the first Greek colonists, Thrace did not have any major cities, exactly as was the case in southern Ukraine. Raiding the village of a rival tribe was a normal activity for a semi-nomad Thracian community, since skirmishes and small-scale local wars were a great occasion to enlarge herds by capturing sheep and goats from their enemy. The territory of Thrace, mostly covered by hills, was not well suited to armies equipped with heavy armour and moving in close formations. The only way to move rapidly and fight effectively in these lands was to act as skirmishers, equipped with throwing weapons and trained in light infantry tactics. The territory of present-day Bulgaria (ancient Thrace), however, also includes some plains, where the Thracians could breed horses and where some excellent cavalry contingents were raised. The Thracian tribes were distinguished between those of the mountains and those of the plains, according to the morphology of the hills or valleys on which they lived. According to ancient authors such as Herodotus, the Thracians were the most numerous people of Europe: if united into a single kingdom, they could have defeated and conquered all the ancient nations living along their borders. Luckily for their neighbours, however, the Thracians always preferred inter-tribal warfare to invasions directed against foreign peoples. Potentially, thanks to their great military capabilities, they could have been one of the leading powers of Antiquity.

By the end of the Greek Dark Ages, around 650 BC, the Thracians were already famous throughout the Mediterranean world for their combat skills and unrivalled courage on the battlefield, as a result of which they started to be employed on a large scale as mercenaries by several ancient kingdoms. In Thrace, the profession of warrior was highly honoured, being considered as superior to all others. Showing courage in battle was fundamental for a Thracian man to acquire a solid reputation. Generally speaking, however, Thracian warriors were not famed for their martial discipline: they loved plunder more than anything else, which frequently caused them serious problems during a battle or campaign. Thracians only obeyed strong war leaders originating from their own tribes, so it was particularly difficult for foreign commanders to secure their loyalty. When serving as mercenaries, if not paid properly and on time, they were prone to mutinies and revolts. Indeed, it was not uncommon for them to switch sides is an enemy leader offered them large amounts of gold or a good opportunity to plunder a rich city. The Thracians never lost their original character of semi-nomadic raiders, even after centuries of close contact with the major civilizations of the Mediterranean. Nothing was more important for them than personal wealth, every possible method of augmenting this being considered as legitimate. Well known for their cruelty, they were also famous for being high-spirited: singing and dancing were two important components of their daily life, together with drinking wine in large quantities. It should be pointed out, however, that their way of life was not so different from that of many other ancient peoples and that their technological skills were by no means rudimentary. They were able to produce deadly metal weapons, as well as working tools. While the Thracians were not used to living in urban centres or to practicing commerce on a large scale, their simple economy was solid enough to provoke frequent demographical booms.

In 513 BC, after completing the preparation of his troops, Darius I crossed into Europe and started ravaging Thrace. He did not meet strong resistance from the Thracian tribes, who preferred to avoid direct confrontation with the Persians. The Thracian leaders soon understood that the Persian troops had come to the Balkans to attack the Scythians north of the Danube and not to occupy their lands. To avoid bloodshed, several Thracian chieftains formally agreed to submit to the Persians, believing that this act would have had no practical future consequences for them (for example, the payment of tributes and sending of military contingents). However, other Thracian warlords harassed the marching Persians by launching surprise attacks with hit-and-run light infantry tactics, which caused significant losses to Darius' troops but could not stop the Persian advance. After crossing the Danube practically unopposed, the Persians entered Scythian territory. At this point the ruler of the Scythians, Idanthyrsus, summoned the monarchs of all the peoples living around his realm to a meeting during which the kings of the northern Balkans decided how to deal with the Achaemenid invasion. Idanthyrsus wanted to form a large-scale anti-Persian alliance, but his attempts ended in political failure, with both the Agathyrsi and the Tauri refusing to support the Scythians in the war against Darius. During the previous decades, the Scythians had expanded their lands across south-western

Side view of a Scythian heavy cavalryman. (*Photo and copyright by Scythian State*)

Side view of a Scythian heavy cavalryman. (*Photo and copyright by Amages Drachen*)

Ukraine and had reached the Danube, thereby depriving the Agathyrsi of most of their lands, so it was understandable that they sided with the Persians in the hope of regaining their recently lost territory. The decision of the Tauri was also a logical one, as both the Scythians and the Greeks were at that time common enemies of the Persians and the Tauri. Facing a massive invasion and having no strong allies, Idanthyrsus mobilized all his forces and started to fight the invaders in the traditional manner of the Eurasian steppes, avoiding any direct confrontation with the enemy and employing a scorched earth strategy. The Scythians evaded the pursuing Persians using feints and retreated eastwards across the Pontic Steppe, attacking them with hit-and-run guerrilla tactics. They devastated the countryside that the Persians had to cross, blocked wells, intercepted convoys in the rear of the enemy, destroyed pastureland and ambushed isolated Achaemenid contingents. The Persians soon started to experience serious difficulties, since they were not used to fighting in the steppe; they began running out of supplies and clean water, while pursuing an enemy that vanished every time they tried to intercept them. The Scythians had no major settlements where the Persians could stop and establish a base, and their knowledge of their homeland meant the Achaemenid troops had no idea where their forces were hidden. According to ancient writers, a highly frustrated Darius sent a letter to Idanthyrsus in which he accused him of being a coward who lacked the courage to fight the Persians on the open field. Idanthyrsus responded that he was just waging war in his own traditional way, like the Scythians had done for centuries. Time and space were important factors that worked in favour of the Scythians, as Darius could not spend too many months away from his empire to campaign in the Pontic Steppe. The invading Persian army survived only thanks to the supplies transported across the Black Sea by their navy, and after several weeks of marching in southern Ukraine Darius was obliged to suspend the advance of his troops. The Persians reached the banks of the Volga River and built eight forts there before starting their return journey. The forts, garrisoned by Persian soldiers, were presumably destroyed by the Scythians soon after Darius left. The Persian retreat across the eastern Balkans was long and difficult, the Achaemenid troops being attacked by Thracian tribes. Before returning to Asia Minor, Darius formally organized Thrace as a new satrapy known as Skudra, which he intended to use as a bridgehead for a future invasion of Greece. As soon as the bulk of the Persian troops had left their homeland, however, most of the Thracian tribes rose up in revolt, skirmishing with the tiny military garrisons that the Persians had left behind in the Balkans. The Persian invasion of Scythia had ended in total failure for Darius, but had also caused serious problems for the Scythians, with some of the most fertile areas of their homeland being ravaged.

Back view of a Scythian heavy cavalryman. (*Photo and copyright by Scythian State*)

Detail of the embroidered hood worn by a Scythian heavy cavalryman. (*Photo and copyright by Amages Drachen*)

# Chapter 3

# The Scythians and the Greco-Persian Wars

After the Achaemenid invasion of 513 BC, both the Scythians and the Thracians returned to their previous political condition, but the Persians started to consider those territories that they had temporarily conquered as part of their empire and organized another expedition to retake them. In 499 BC, a first Persian expedition was mounted against the Greeks, and in particular against the island of Naxos. The invasion was organized by one of the Greek tyrants of Asia Minor who were loyal to Persia, Aristagoras of Miletus, but included the participation of a sizeable Achaemenid military force. The attack against Naxos, however, was a failure: after a siege lasting four months, the Persians abandoned the island, having suffered severe losses. They had underestimated the capabilities of the Greeks and had revealed their own military weakness. Meanwhile, before they could plan any further expedition, their former Milesian allies, guided by Aristagoras, rose up in rebellion. This was the beginning of the Ionian Revolt, a conflict that changed forever the relations between the peoples of the eastern Mediterranean. Several Greek cities of Asia Minor had already assembled their forces in Myus in order to support the Persian efforts against Naxos, but when news of the Milesian revolt reached Myus, the Greek soldiers mutinied and joined the rebellion. Aristagoras presented himself as the leader of the Asian Greeks in the struggle against the Persians and ordered the arrest of most of the other tyrants, as a result of which most of the Asian *poleis* rapidly became free from indirect Persian control and transformed themselves into democracies. Aristagoras was even able to capture the large fleet that the Persians had assembled to attack Naxos, so the Achaemenids found themselves with no naval forces in the Aegean. The tyrants installed by the Persians were unable to control the situation: differently from those of mainland Greece, they were not popular leaders, just loyal officials who ruled on behalf of their Achaemenid masters. In the winter of 499 BC, in view of the anticipated Persian counter-attack, Aristagoras went to mainland Greece in search of allies. He knew that the Persians would soon return with a new fleet and army, and he was in desperate need of reinforcement. Aristagoras tried unsuccessfully to create an alliance with the Spartans, then went to Athens, a city that was already hostile to the Persians. In recent years, Hippias, a former tyrant of Athens who had been removed by the populace, had become a member of the

Achaemenid court and had been able to gain the support of his new protectors. In the years preceding the outbreak of the Ionian Revolt, the Persians had ordered the Athenians to accept Hippias back as their tyrant, but the city refused and from that moment on they considered themselves to be at war with the Persian Empire.

Scythian heavy cavalryman. (*Photo and copyright by Scythian State*)

Scythian heavy cavalryman. (*Photo and copyright by Amages Drachen*)

Aristagoras was thus able to gain unconditioned support from the Athenians. The city of Athens, with its new democratic government, had already been a model for the *poleis* of Asia Minor in their struggle against tyrants imposed upon them, and furthermore, Athens was an Ionian city, just like most of those that were now rebelling against the Persians. The city of Eretria also agreed to help Aristagoras, probably in exchange for the support received from Miletus during a previous war. The Athenians sent a total of twenty triremes to support the rebels in Asia Minor, while the Eretrians despatched a smaller contingent of five warships.

The Greek army of Asia, reinforced by the Athenians and Eretrians, assembled at Ephesus before marching against the capital of the Persian province of Lydia. Taken by surprise, the Persians were unable to organize a proper defence, and after a brief assault the Greeks occupied Sardes in the heart of Anatolia. The Persian garrison of the city, however, was not destroyed, resisting in the citadel under the command of Artaphernes. When the lower city accidentally caught fire, it forced the Persians to come out from the citadel to avoid being burned to death. Against the odds, their desperate counter-attack was successful and the Greeks were obliged to retreat from Sardes. Nevertheless, most of the city was destroyed. This episode persuaded the Persians that the revolt was a serious affair and they started to assemble a large army to re-establish their control of the region. Meanwhile, the demoralized Greeks returned to their starting positions in Ephesus. Artaphernes organized a large cavalry force in central Anatolia, with which he was able to intercept the retreating Greeks on the outskirts of Ephesus. During the ensuing battle, the Greek army was completely routed and suffered many casualties, the few surviving Athenians and Eretrians going back to their ships and quickly retreating to mainland Greece. The Greeks of Asia, however, continued to put up fierce resistance, the revolt spreading to other Persian domains around the Aegean Sea. The Greeks sent expeditions against the cities located on the Hellespont and the Dardanelles that were under Persian political influence in order to assume control over these strategic areas. By 494 BC, the Persians had mustered a massive army in central Anatolia and were ready to launch a final offensive against the Greeks of Asia. A new Achaemenid fleet had also been assembled, with which to supply the land forces. The Persian army moved directly against Miletus and besieged it. Meanwhile, the Greeks of Asia decided not to fight on land against the invaders but to embark their forces on all the warships that were available. The Greek fleet was assembled at the island of Lade, near the coast of Miletus, waiting for the right moment to attack the Persian warships. The Greeks had a total of 353 triremes, an impressive number for the standards of the time. Nevertheless, when the naval clash finally took place it turned into a disaster for the Greeks, who suffered a decisive defeat, many of their warships changing sides during

Scythian heavy cavalryman firing with his composite bow. (*Photo and copyright by Amages Drachen*)

the battle. Thereafter, Miletus was stormed and destroyed by the Persian army, which was a terrible blow for the many city colonies established in Crimea. By 493 BC, the great Ionian Revolt was practically over. The Persians occupied the islands of Chios, Lesbos and Tenedos, which had played an important role in the last part of the rebellion, and were thus now extremely near to the borders of mainland Greece. The Persian retaliation against the Greek cities of Asia Minor was terrible, but did not last for long as they did not want to permanently damage the economic capabilities of such a rich region of their empire. Furthermore, instead of restoring the old tyrants to power, the Persians accepted the new democratic forms of government that had emerged in most of the Greek urban centres.

Scythian light cavalryman. (*Photo and copyright by Scythian State*)

In 492 BC, the Persians organized a new expedition directed against the Thracians and the Scythians, with the objective of re-establishing their control over the European regions that they had temporarily invaded during 513 BC. This was probably intended as a preliminary operation to a future offensive against Greece, for which the Persian army needed to have a base on the European continent. The Achaemenid expeditionary corps of 492 BC was guided by Mardonius, son-in-law of Darius I, and departed from the Anatolian region of Cilicia. The Persian army advanced by land to the Hellespont in northern Anatolia, marching along the coastline in order to retain direct contact with the fleet. At this point all the troops were embarked on the ships and crossed the Hellespont without any particular problems. Once in Europe, the Persians focused on re-subjugating the Thracian tribes one by one. Indeed, since the tribes were politically divided, the occupation of southern Thrace was not a difficult task for Mardonius. At this point of the campaign, instead of moving north to fight against the Scythians, the Persians marched west in order to enter Greece from the north. Memories of the defeat suffered in Scythia were still fresh in Persia, and it is highly probable that Darius had ordered the army not to waste time by trying to subjugate the warlike Scythians. The Persians soon reached Macedonia, a semi-barbarous Greek kingdom of little political and military importance at the time. The Macedonians were under a mix of influences, part Greek, Illyrian and Thracian. During the expedition of 513 BC, they had already recognized the Persians as their overlords, and they did the same in 492 BC. Everything seemed to work well for Mardonius until the Persian fleet was surprised by a terrible storm, which destroyed most of its 300 ships. The Persian navy had little knowledge of that part of the Aegean, and the disaster could have probably been avoided. Whatever the case, the land forces were now left alone. Shortly afterwards, the large Persian camp in Macedonia was attacked by one of the strongest Thracian tribes, the Brygians, who had still to be fully subjugated. The surprise assault caused serious losses to the Achaemenids and Mardonius was wounded. At this point, having no support from the fleet, Mardonius decided to go back to Asia Minor with all his forces, crossing the Hellespont in what remained of his warships. Before leaving, however, the Persians crushed the Brygians and left some garrisons in Thrace and Macedonia. The European campaign of Mardonius had been a half-failure, but it had secured for the Persians the land approaches to the Greek mainland. In 491 BC, sensing that the Greeks had been greatly impressed by his campaign in Thrace and Macedonia, Darius decided that the time had come to also annex mainland Greece to his immense empire.

During the Persian Wars of 490–479 BC, the Scythians had looked with favour on the Greeks, providing them latter with large amounts of grain and natural resources, which were exported through the commercial networks of the Greek colonies in

Crimea (most of which were allied with Athens). It is interesting to note that during the Persian Wars, the light troops of the Athenian army included a special force of 'Scythian' archers, which was raised in 490 BC and comprised some 300 soldiers. There are very few precise details about this exotic military unit in Athenian service, but what is known for sure is that it was made up of foreigners who were slaves in Athens. Considering that the corps was formed shortly after the Battle of Marathon, it is probable that these 'Scythian' archers came from the many Persian prisoners captured by the Athenians at Marathon. Some sources, however, state that the original 300 archers were all slaves bought from the Black Sea region by the Athenian government. At that time, it was common practice for the Athenians to buy large numbers of slaves from Thrace and the Black Sea region. Whatever the truth, since their recruitment the 'Scythian' archers had acted as an elite police corps inside the city of Athens. They were equipped as soldiers with the traditional composite bow employed by the Scythians, but mostly performed police duties, their main function being to maintain order during public gatherings and to act as watchmen or guards for public buildings. From a legal point of view, they were public slaves and thus property of the Athenian government. The 300 Scythian archers were separated from the other Athenian archers of the army, who performed regular military functions and numbered some 1,200 in total. As time progressed, the original 300 'Scythian' archers started to be replaced by other public slaves of foreign nationality, who continued to be dressed and equipped as Scythians. Using foreign slaves as policemen was likely the result of a precise choice, since they did not have any link with the political parties of Athens and thus were completely neutral in performing their duties – a citizen or an Athenian slave could easily have been influenced by one of the factions that fought for power. We have no idea when the Scythian archers were finally disbanded, but this probably happened in 395 BC.

Following the end of the Persian Wars, the political situation of the Balkans changed in a significant way. The Athenians started to enact an aggressive foreign policy and one of its main objectives was obtaining direct control over the trade routes crossing the Black Sea. At the same time, the Scythians tried to take advantage of the Persians' defeat by expanding south of the Danube. Already in 496 BC, a large Scythian army had crossed the river and had attacked Thrace; the Thracians, taken by surprise, were not able to organize an effective resistance and could do very little to prevent the raiding of their homeland. The Scythians reached as far as the Chersonese, plundering dozens of Thracian villages and capturing thousands of Thracian individuals who were enslaved. The Scythian invasion of 496 BC demonstrated to the Thracians how their political fragmentation made them quite weak militarily. Without joining their forces, the Thracians could never have prevented the conquest of their homeland

Scythian horse archer. (*Photo and copyright by Amages Drachen*)

Back view of a Scythian horse archer. (*Photo and copyright by Scythian State*)

from the Scythians. As a result of the above, a first independent and unified kingdom started to emerge in Thrace around 470 BC. It was created by a very capable leader named Teres, who headed one of the most important Thracian tribes, the Odrysians. These lived in the fertile plain of the Hebrus River and were extremely numerous, being famous for their combat capabilities and always being one of the leading Thracian tribes. Under the guidance of Teres, they were able to impose their will on most of the communities living in present-day Bulgaria, unifying the region as the Odrysian Kingdom. Under Sitalces, the successor of Teres, the new state reached its greatest territorial extent and stopped the Scythian incursions directed south of the Danube. The new border between the Scythian territories and the Odrysian Kingdom was set as the Danube, after which relations between the Thracians and the Scythians greatly improved. During the following decades, for example, it was not uncommon for a member of the Odrysian royal family to marry a Scythian princess.

After Sitalces' death, however, the Odrysian Kingdom experienced serious internal difficulties, many of the tribes starting to revolt against the Odrysians and a new age of political fragmentation beginning.

The unified state had never had a centralized organization, its existence having always been based on the military supremacy of the Odrysians. The latter had exerted control over most of Thrace for a period, but for some areas of the country this was only nominal. The majority of the Thracian tribes did not want to live in a centralized state, considering the other communities of their same people as traditional enemies. The brief experience of the Odrysian Kingdom was unable to counter the endemic inter-tribal rivalries that had always damaged the social development of the Thracians. During Sitalces' reign, the Thracians had been a great military power of the Balkans: in the north, they had stopped Scythian expansionism on the Danube, while in the south-west, they had formed military alliances with the Greeks and had participated in the Peloponnesian War fought between Athens and Sparta. Sitalces, also known as Sitalces the Great because of his many victories, decided to side with Athens during this wide-ranging conflict, and thus fought against the Spartans and their allies. In 429 BC, the Odrysian Kingdom assembled a large army of over 150,000 warriors and invaded Macedonia, which was an ally of Sparta during the Peloponnesian War. The Thracians were able to conquer Macedonia after a brief campaign, and then moved south in order to seize the Greek cities that were located in the Chalcidian Peninsula and that supported Sparta. According to the plans that had been agreed with the Athenians, Sitalces' large army would be supported by the Athenian navy during the difficult siege operations of the Chalcidian cities. When the Thracians arrived in the Chalcidian Peninsula, however, they found no Athenians to assist them. Apparently, the Athenians had been so impressed by the rapid invasion of Macedonia that they now considered the Thracians a great potential menace with an army of 150,000 barbarian warriors who could have easily occupied most of Greece after conquering the Chalcidian cities. After pillaging the Chalcidian Peninsula for several days, but being unable to besiege the Greek cities without Athenian war machines, the Thracians went back to their homeland with enormous amounts of looted gold. In 424 BC, Sitalces the Great died while fighting an internal war against the tribe of the Triballi (who had never been part of a unified Thrace), after which his realm was divided into several smaller kingdoms ruled by different members of the Odrysian royal family. The ensuing sudden collapse of the Odrysian Kingdom favoured the rapid resurgence of Macedonia in the heart of the Balkans and led to an increase of Greek influence over Thrace. As anticipated above, the Triballi had never been part of the Odrysian Kingdom. They were considered as the most barbarian of all Thracians by the Greeks, and were settled on the north-western border of Thrace. Here they lived in a state of constant war against the Scythians in the north and the Illyrians in the west. The Triballi gradually acquired several cultural features of their enemies and thereby started to be considered as something different from the usual

Thracians. After the fall of the Odrysian Kingdom, two Thracian tribes assumed a prominent political and military role: the Triballi, who conquered large territories in the heart of the Balkans at the expenses of the Macedonians, and the Getae. The Getae were settled around the Danube delta in north-eastern Thrace, where they lived in a constant state of war against the Scythians and became famous as horse-breeders. The cavalry of the Getae had a lot in common with that of the Scythians, and was considered to be the best in Thrace. Most of the Greeks did not consider the Getae to be part of the Thracians, as they had been heavily influenced by the Scythians from a cultural point of view and they had a distinct religion that was quite different from that of the other Thracian tribes. Nevertheless, the social structures and the main traditions of the Getae were clearly Thracian. The golden age of the

Scythian horse archer firing with his composite bow. (*Photo and copyright by Amages Drachen*)

Scythian horse archer firing with his composite bow. (*Photo and copyright by Scythian State*)

Triballi and the Getae, however, lasted only a few decades, because from 359 BC a new power started to emerge in the heart of the Balkans: the Kingdom of Macedonia.

For a long time, Macedonia was not considered to be part of the Greek world, since it was located on the northern edge of the Hellenic world and its inhabitants were quite different from those of the great Greek urban centres like Athens or Sparta. The Macedonians spoke Greek and practiced the same religion as the southern Greeks, but had a completely different lifestyle. Their main difference was that they did not live in large cities like most other Greeks, their settlements being dispersed across a vast countryside and consisting of small rural villages. In addition, the Macedonian economy and society were completely different from those of the Greeks: commerce and craftsmanship were quite underdeveloped, since the local economy was based on agriculture and animal breeding. These were the main occupations of the Macedonians, the majority of whom were free men who owned a small farm, sustaining their families with the products of their land and large flocks of sheep or goats. The breeding of horses was also particularly important for the economy of Macedonia, as they were employed for war and could also be sold to the southern Greeks in exchange for significant sums of money. Macedonian society retained a very tribal nature for a long time, the development of a centralized state being extremely slow compared to the rest of the Greek world. Each village was dominated by its own noble warlord, who was at the head of a personal retinue of warriors. No form of democracy existed and the king exerted only nominal power over the land's many nobles. These nobles and their warriors fought as horsemen and were extremely warlike, pillaging and raiding being common activities. Macedonia had very few slaves and all the subjects of the king were free men, but between them and the aristocracy there was no middle class. Culturally, the Macedonians could not be compared with the Greeks: they spoke Greek with a distinctive 'rural' accent and did not practice philosophy like the Athenians. Macedonian civilization was in essence a simplified version of the Greek one, to the point that the Greeks considered the Macedonians as semi-barbarians who had very little in common with them. This was partly true, because the Kingdom of Macedonia was located in the heart of the Balkans and thus was heavily influenced by the nearby civilizations of the Thracians and Illyrians, who frequently invaded or raided Macedonia, obliging the kingdom to live in state of continuous turmoil.

This political situation, which was characterized by a high level of anarchy, came to an end only in 392 BC when Amyntas III assumed power as the new king of Macedonia. The father of Philip II and grandfather of Alexander the Great, Amyntas is now considered as the real founder of the unified Kingdom of Macedonia. He was a very skilled diplomat and formed a wide network of alliances between his realm and the other powers of the southern Balkans, his allies including Athens, Thessaly, the Chalcidian League and the Odrysians. At that time, the major external threat to the Macedonians was represented by the Illyrians, who were trying to expand their dominions southwards, but thanks to Amyntas' diplomatic moves, Macedonia retained its territorial integrity and all the nobles of the realm were brought back under direct control of the court. Amyntas III's direct successor was his eldest son, Alexander II, who had great difficulty in keeping order in Macedonia due to the outbreak of a civil war. This conflict was only resolved by Athens' military intervention in support of Alexander II, who defeated his rival Pausanias. The new Macedonian king tried to expand his realm's sphere of influence by intervening in the internal politics of Thessaly, which at the time was ravaged by civil war. The Macedonians occupied a large portion of northern Thessaly, but this audacious move was soon punished by the city of Thebes, then the dominant military power in Greece. After having been defeated by the superior Theban forces, Alexander II was forced to abandon Thessaly and to become a loyal ally of Thebes. He also had to send his younger brother, Philip (the future father of Alexander the Great), as a royal hostage to Thebes. Alexander II was succeeded by Amyntas III's second son, Perdiccas III, who tried to reconquer from the Illyrians some lands that had

Detail of war hammer and knife carried by a Scythian light cavalryman. (*Photo and copyright by Amages Drachen*)

been previously lost by the Macedonians but was killed during one of his military campaigns. Perdiccas III's sudden death in 359 BC caused great political trouble in Pella, the Macedonian capital, the kingdom's nobles choosing the infant son of the monarch as their new king rather than Philip. However, Philip soon became the tutor and regent of the infant, and within months he proclaimed himself king and dethroned his young nephew.

In 359 BC, at the age of 23, Philip II became supreme ruler of Macedonia during the most difficult period in the history of his realm. After the sudden death of Perdiccas, the enemies of the Macedonians had formed a strong military alliance and invaded Philip's new kingdom by taking advantage of the political chaos that reigned in Pella. The Illyrians raided the north-west of Macedonia, while a joint force of Paeonians and Thracians pillaged the eastern half of the country. At the

Scythian horse archer preparing his composite bow for use. (*Photo and copyright by Scythian State*)

same time, the Athenians landed a military contingent just south of Macedonia to support a pretender to the throne by the name of Argeus. Pressed by enemies on all sides and being in a very weak military position, Philip had no choice but to employ diplomacy to slow down the actions of his enemies. He halted the raids of the Paeonians and Thracians by promising to pay a tribute to them, thereby gaining precious time to mobilize his forces. Meanwhile, he married the daughter of the most important Illyrian warlord, Bardylis of the Dardanians, who had been able to unite several southern Illyrian communities into a single kingdom and had defeated the Macedonian army of Perdiccas III. Being in no condition to face the Dardanians on equal terms, Philip preferred to form an alliance with them through his marriage. After thus stabilizing the military situation on his northern borders, he marched against the 3,000 Athenian hoplites who had landed south of Macedonia and eliminated the pretender Argeus after obtaining a decisive victory in battle. In a time of terrible crisis, Philip had been able to preserve the territorial integrity of his realm, but it was clear to him that he would soon be obliged to fight against those tribes that still represented a threat to the borders of Macedonia. Indeed, hostilities resumed between the Macedonians and the Illyrians in 358 BC, Philip finding it unacceptable that the Illyrians were still in control of a large portion of northern Macedonia. The young warrior king mobilized every able-bodied man of his realm and marched against Bardylis. The decisive clash of this new war took place in the Erigon Valley, when for the first time the famous Macedonian phalanx was deployed in battle. The encounter ended with a brilliant victory for Philip, the first of his incredible career; some 7,000 Illyrians were killed, including Bardylis.

Following Philip's unexpected success, the Macedonians could reconquer the north-western portion of their realm and establish a new frontier line with the Dardanians along the shores of Lake Ohrid. The new border could be defended much more easily by the Macedonians than the previous one, and remained unchanged for many years. Philip, however, soon had to face a new menace on the northern frontier of his kingdom, as during the previous years, a powerful king named Ateas had emerged from the Scythians living north of the Danube and had reunited them after a period of political fragmentation. The Scythian monarch was extremely ambitious and had plans to expand the territory of his people towards the heart of the Balkans. By 340 BC, the Scythians already posed a serious threat to Macedonia, challenging its dominance over Thrace and Illyria. In 339 BC, Ateas launched an invasion of Macedonian lands at the head of a large army. Philip responded by moving north with his troops, and the opposing armies met on the plains of Dobruja in modern north-eastern Romania. According to ancient sources, the ensuing clash was extremely violent, the Scythian horse archers having to face the battle-hardened Macedonian phalangites (pikemen

Detail of a Scythian quiver with composite bow and arrows. (*Photo and copyright by Amages Drachen*)

fighting in a phalanx) on the open field for the first time. The reformed army of Philip II, despite the great courage of its enemies, obtained a stunning victory, with several thousand Scythian warriors being killed, among them Ateas. The Scythians thereafter moved north of the Danube and abandoned their expansionist ambitions. For Philip, however, victory had been costly, his army suffering significant losses and the monarch himself being badly wounded during the battle. After securing his position in the north, Philip understood that his excellent troops could enable him to transform Macedonia into the superpower of the Hellenic world. In less than two decades, he was able to subdue virtually all of Greece, an achievement that had seemed impossible when he became king. Dominating the southern Balkans,

Detail of the embroidered hood worn by a Scythian light cavalryman. (*Photo and copyright by Scythian State*)

however, was not enough for him, and in 336 BC a Macedonian expeditionary force of 10,000 soldiers landed in Asia Minor, being welcomed by the local Greeks who revolted against their Persian governors. Before any decisive fighting could take place between the Macedonians and the Persians, however, Philip was assassinated.

Following Philip II's death, the various cities and tribes that had been submitted by the Macedonians during the previous decades rose up in revolt against his son and heir, Alexander. Many of the Macedonians' enemies were convinced that the new king was too young to rule the territories conquered by his father. Athens, Thebes, Thessaly and the Thracians all rebelled against Alexander, but the young monarch responded by rapidly mobilizing his cavalry and moving to restore order in his dominions. He first attacked the Thessalians, finding them encamped in a strategic pass located between Mount Olympos and Mount Ossa. In order to surprise his enemies, Alexander ordered part of his heavy cavalry to ride over Mount Ossa and deploy to the rear of the Thessalians. Realizing they were surrounded, the Thessalians decided to surrender and immediately joined the Macedonian forces. After regaining control of Thessaly and most of the rest of Greece, the young king turned his attention towards Thrace. Here, starting from the spring of 335 BC, he mounted a full-scale invasion to defeat the Triballi, his main opponents in that region. The Thracian light troops were superior to those of Alexander, but the phalangites and heavy cavalry of the Macedonian army were invincible, leading Alexander to a clear victory over the Thracians in a bloody pitched battle. After crushing the Triballi and forcing them to move north of the Danube, Alexander attacked the Getae along his realm's northern border. As we have seen, while of Thracian stock, the Getae were under a strong Scythian influence, their military forces including heavily armoured horsemen and mounted archers exactly like those of the Scythians. In order to crush the Getae, Alexander decided to cross the Danube: he was the first Macedonian monarch to attempt such an audacious move, but his boldness was rewarded. The Getae were heavily defeated and obliged to move north into the territories of the Scythians.

During his brilliant northern campaign of 335 BC, Alexander came into contact with the Celtic communities that had been living in the heart of the Balkans for decades. These tribes had been particularly impressed by the military achievements of the Macedonian king and had a very positive attitude towards him, since the Thracians defeated by Alexander were their main enemies. After his victory over the Getae, Alexander decided to encamp near the Danube with his army, where he received embassies sent by all the peoples of the region, including those of the Celts. Each tribe then agreed to submit, at least formally, to the Macedonian king. Thanks to Arrian, a formidable ancient source, we know some interesting details about the meeting that took place between Alexander and the Celtic ambassadors. In

Detail of the arrows carried inside a Scythian quiver. (*Photo and copyright by Amages Drachen*)

the words of the Greek writer, the Celts were 'men of haughty demeanour and tall in proportion'; they came to the Macedonian camp with no intention to submit, but just to recognize Alexander as a capable military leader. The Celtic delegation wanted to offer their people's friendship and to reach an agreement that would be positive for both sides. The Balkan Celts hoped to avoid war with the Macedonians, but they had no intention to discuss peace terms from a position of weakness. Alexander had different ideas, considering himself to be no mere monarch but the descendant of the legendary Achilles. In order to test the temperament of the Celts, of whom he knew quite little, the Macedonian king asked their representatives what they feared most in the world. He expected that the response would have been along the lines of: 'You, great Alexander!' Arrian says the Celts, instead, surprised him with an answer that perfectly reflected their mentality: 'We fear only that the sky falls and crushes

Scythian horse archer. (*Photo and copyright by Amages Drachen*)

us or that the earth opens and swallows us or that the sea rises and overwhelms us.' The Celts had essentially answered that they feared nothing, except for the power of nature. Initially, Alexander was infuriated by this response, but he soon understood that the Celts could have answered no other way: they were a people of free and courageous warriors, the kind of men he had always admired. Consequently, a peace treaty was concluded between the Macedonians and the Celts that was positive for both sides. Alexander proclaimed himself as the 'friend of the Celts' and promised that he would never invade their lands. Before returning south, the young king marched into Illyria and defeated two local rulers who were ready to resume their raids against Macedonia. In an extremely rapid and effective campaign, Alexander had been able to secure the northern borders of his realm and had decisively defeated the two most powerful Thracian tribes. The Danube now marked the frontier between Macedonian possessions and the barbarian northern lands inhabited by the Scythians. The latter had a very difficult relationship with Alexander, as they had with his father Philip II. During the early part of Philip's reign, he had been an ally of the Scythians, but in 342 BC he conducted a short campaign against their communities settled south of the Danube, who supported his Thracian enemies. Alexander did not campaign against the Scythians, but against their Getae allies. The Scythians, however, considered the Kingdom of Macedonia as a great potential threat to the territorial integrity of their domains, and when Alexander invaded the Achaemenid Empire they provided the Persians with substantial numbers of mercenaries (both heavy cavalrymen and horse archers). These fought in the decisive Battle of Gaugamela in 331 BC, where they formed the core of the Persian heavy cavalry.

After defeating the Persian Emperor Darius III at Gaugamela, Alexander invaded southern Mesopotamia and occupied Babylon. The Macedonians entered the city in triumph and discovered a new world: the fabulous city, famous for its gardens and religious buildings, had before then been visited by just a few Greek merchants. The first of the four Persian capitals had fallen and was soon followed by the second, the magnificent city of Susa that was located in Elam, on the eastern borders of modern Kuwait. Despite having been soundly defeated and lost two of his richest cities, Darius still had no intention of surrendering, as he continued to exert control over the eastern half of the Persian Empire, which comprised the heartland of his people (Iran) and several other provinces stretching south to India and north to Central Asia. All these lands were inhabited by warlike peoples, so Darius could easily recruit another army. In addition, some Achaemenid troops had been able to escape from the battlefield of Gaugamela and had followed their monarch: 1,000 Bactrian cataphracts (heavy cavalry) commanded by Bessus, half of the Immortals (elite heavy infantry) and 2,000 Greek mercenaries. For the first time in this campaign, Darius now acted rapidly, sending letters to all his eastern satraps ordering them to mobilize their forces and giving a speech in front of his remaining soldiers in order to boost their morale. The Achaemenid monarch then moved to Ecbatana, in the Zagros Mountains of Iran, where he started putting together a new army. To mobilize a sufficient number of men and organize them correctly, however, Darius needed time, to gain which he left behind 3,000 of his best remaining soldiers with orders to slow down Alexander's movements for as long as possible. These chosen soldiers were under command of Ariobarzanes, one of the most experienced Persian generals. To enter Iran, the Macedonians had to march on the so-called Royal Road, a Persian highway built several decades before by Darius I which connected Susa with the two eastern capitals of the Achaemenids, Persepolis and Pasargadae. The

The personal equipment of a Scythian horse archer. (*Photo and copyright by Amages Drachen*)

Scythian horse archer. (*Photo and copyright by Amages Drachen*)

terrain surrounding the Royal Road was covered by mountains and marching across it during winter was hazardous, especially for an army that had little knowledge of the region that it was crossing. The Zagros Mountains marked the border between Mesopotamia and Persia (Iran); only a few roads crossed them and these all went through narrow mountain passes. Ariobarzanes had a detailed knowledge of the area and believed he could defend the passes for months with his few elite troops, providing Darius with the time he had asked for to raise a new army.

After capturing Susa, Alexander continued his advance by dividing his army in two parts: one, under the command of Parmenion, moved along the Royal Road; the other, under his own leadership, tried to cross the Zagros Mountains by traversing a narrow mountain pass known as the Persian Gate. The latter could easily be defended by a small number of men and was the perfect location for an ambush. During his advance, Alexander had to fight various local tribes such as the Uxians, who attacked him with hit-and-run tactics. Meanwhile, Ariobarzanes and his Persians prepared an ambush in the Persian Gate, which was preceded by a valley that was very wide in its initial part but progressively narrowed before reaching the mountain pass. Understanding that the Macedonians had little knowledge of the terrain, the Persians deployed on the two slopes surrounding the Persian Gate and built a wall to block the pass. At its narrowest point, the pass was just a couple of metres wide, and it was here that the Persians planned to ambush Alexander and his men, who probably numbered less than 10,000. Ariobarzanes' plan worked perfectly, the Macedonians being attacked while crossing the Persian Gate and suffering severe losses under a rain of arrows and boulders. Unable to press on, Alexander was forced to fall back in order to reorganize his forces. During the following four weeks, the Persians defended the mountain pass with great determination, similarly to how the Spartan hoplites had fought in the Pass of Thermopylae during the Second Persian War. Ariobarzanes wanted to stop Alexander until the coming of spring, and had the resources to do so. The Macedonian king, however, was well aware of the risk that he was running in the heart of the Zagros Mountains, so decided to carry out one of his trademark manoeuvres: he organized a complex pincer attack, sending some of his best light infantry to climb over the two hills that surrounded the Persian Gate. The defenders were then taken by surprise and crushed after a very harsh fight. Ariobarzanes had been sure that the Macedonians would be unable to find a path across the hills to attack him on the flanks. Apparently, Alexander had been able to employ some Persian prisoners as guides and thus found a way to encircle the defenders in the pass. At the cost of heavy casualties, the Macedonians had finally conquered the Persian Gate, the defeat of Ariobarzanes removing the last military obstacle between Alexander and Persepolis. The Macedonians were then able to capture Persepolis with ease, as they did at Pasargadae, at the same time taking possession of Darius' treasury, which was considered to be the richest in the ancient world. Surprised by Alexander's ability to pass through the Persian Gate, Darius had to abandon Ecbatana and move even further east in order to continue his general mobilization.

After the Macedonians prevailed at the Persian Gate, Darius went to the eastern satrapies of Bactria and Sogdia, which were ruled by the powerful governor Bessus, who had commanded the left wing of the Persian forces at Gaugamela. Bessus and many of his highly skilled warriors had been able to survive the bloody defeat at Gaugamela, but had fled to Ecbatana with Darius and then followed the king when he moved further east. Darius planned to move to the satrapies of Central Asia so he could raise a new army and gain time to prepare a counter-offensive against Alexander. With the end of winter, the Persians started to be pursued by the Macedonians, who were determined to capture Darius in order to bring the war to an end. While fleeing to Bactria, with Alexander's cavalry in close pursuit, Bessus realized the hopelessness of the Persian position so decided to organize a conspiracy against Darius, together with the other satraps of the Central Asian provinces. The revolt instigated by Bessus was successful, Darius being put in golden chains by the traitors, who hoped that by giving their king to Alexander they could obtain some political advantage and retain their own possessions. The most ambitious of the plotters was Bessus, who wished to replace Darius as the Persian Empire's monarch and probably hoped to obtain control over the vast eastern provinces. The rebel satraps tried to surrender Darius to the Macedonians, but Alexander would accept no agreement and ordered a continuation of the chase of the remaining Persian forces. At this point, Bessus and the other traitors stabbed Darius and left him dying in a chariot that was found by the pursuing Macedonian soldiers. Bessus immediately proclaimed himself King of Persia, adopting the name of Artaxerxes V. From many points of view, his self-proclaimed ascension was logical, since the satrap of Bactria was the nearest noble to Darius' heirs in the line of succession to the Persian throne. When Alexander reached Darius' body with his cavalry, he ordered the burial of the enemy king with full honours and showed great respect for his former rival. Meanwhile, he promised that he would severely punish Darius' killers.

The death of Darius did not lead to an immediate end of the war, which now continued between Alexander and Bessus. The Macedonians began their conquest of Central Asia, which would finally lead them to India. The satrapies of Bactria and Sogdia, which the Macedonians attacked next, were mostly inhabited by nomadic peoples of the steppes, having a lot in common with the Scythians. Indeed, the Scythians had lived for a long time in Central Asia before being forced to migrate to the Pontic Steppe. In 329 BC, the Macedonian army entered Bactria by way of the

Scythian hook used to attach the quiver to the waistbelt. (*Photo and copyright by Amages Drachen*)

Scythian horse archer. (*Photo and copyright by Amages Drachen*)

Hindu Kush mountain range, which had been left undefended by Bessus, who wanted to move his forces further east in order to weaken the morale of the Macedonians and lengthen their supply lines. Having a superior knowledge of the local terrain, Bessus probably had in mind to conduct a guerrilla campaign against Alexander. By causing continuous minor losses to the enemy with guerrilla tactics and by burning crops while retreating, exactly like the Scythians had done against the Persians in 513 BC, Bessus hoped to defeat the Macedonians without having to face them on the battlefield. However, after crossing the Oxus River, which today marks the border between Afghanistan and Tagikistan, the Bactrian mounted troops deserted and abandoned Bessus, who was seized by several of his chieftains and handed over to the pursuing Macedonians. Bessus was then tortured and killed as a punishment for having dethroned the legitimate monarch, Darius III. By this move, Alexander won the support of several Persian nobles who were still loyal to the memory of Darius. The death of Bessus, however, did not mark the end of Alexander's campaign in Central Asia. He had by then conquered almost all the territories of the Persian Empire, but some of the border regions had not yet accepted his rule and continued to resist. Oxyartes, one of the satraps who had betrayed Bessus, became the new leader of the Persian resistance forces. Alexander continued his advance towards the north, into the heart of Central Asia, capturing Samarkand (in modern Uzbekistan) and reaching the River Jaxartes, where he founded the city of Alexandria Eschate (Alexandria the Farthest). Despite these successes, the Macedonians had to face a number of uprisings from the indigenous Sogdian tribesmen, who remained loyal to Oxyartes. These mounted fighters employed with great success their usual hit-and-run tactics against the Macedonians, relying on their mastery of horsemanship and archery to attack the invaders from a distance. During the interminable skirmishes fought against the Sogdians, Alexander lost more soldiers than in any other of his military campaigns. This started to cause general discontent in the Macedonian army, as Alexander's soldiers did not see the point of continuing their conquests in such an insignificant and poor region of the Persian Empire. The first episodes of rebellion soon expanded into mutinies, forcing Alexander for the first time to face internal problems caused by his own troops. The Macedonian leaders had never faced guerrilla warfare before and had to develop new tactics in order to defeat their nomadic enemies. These novel tactics included the combined use of catapults and archers to hit enemy skirmishers operating on high ground, as well as carrying out costly sieges. Meanwhile, the Sogdian mountain strongholds were proving formidable.

Despite being injured on more than one occasion and suffering from dysentery, Alexander was finally able to win a decisive battle against the Sogdians on the River Jaxartes. At that time, Sogdia was inhabited by the Saka, a nomadic steppe people

Detail showing the points of some Scythian arrows. (*Photo and copyright by Amages Drachen*)

speaking a form of Scythian language and being very similar in many respects to the Scythians. Indeed, the Saka were known as the Eastern Scythians by some ancient Greek authors, but thanks to modern research it has been established that they were a distinct people from the Scythians. We have no idea of their historical origins: probably they were the result of a mix between some Scythian communities that remained in Central Asia and the nomadic Massagetae newcomers. The Saka provided major military contingents to the Persian army, and it is possible that the Scythian cavalrymen present at the Battle of Gaugamela were Saka hailing from Sogdia rather than Scythian mercenaries. Whatever the truth, the Saka were among the fiercest enemies ever faced by Alexander the Great during his brilliant military career. With the defeat of their northern tribes, the Sogdians in the south decided to concentrate all their forces at a fortress called the Sogdian Rock, which was located on top of a large escarpment and was considered impossible to conquer by all the inhabitants of Central Asia. The actual site of the Sogdian Rock is still an argument of debate for historians, but the majority of them believe that it was probably located in the surroundings of Samarkand. This defensive position of the Sogdians was very strong, and after arriving at the position Alexander soon understood he could not take it by traditional storm. He worked out that the only way to capture the Sogdian Rock was for a selected group of elite mountaineer troops to use ropes to reach the top of the fortress in order to attack the defenders by surprise. The

Scythian light cavalryman armed with war hammer. (*Photo and copyright by Scythian State*)

Macedonian leader called for volunteers, explaining to his men the difficulties of this special mission. Some 300 men came forward; using ropes and tent pegs, they were to make the ascent during the hours of darkness. Oxyartes had previously sent his wife and daughters to take refuge in the fortress, since he considered the position

Detail of a Scythian dagger. (*Photo and copyright by Amages Drachen*)

Back view of a Scythian light cavalryman armed with war hammer. (*Photo and copyright by Scythian State*)

to be the safest place for his family. The Sogdian Rock did not have a very large garrison, but it was well provisioned for a long siege. Before launching his attack, Alexander had asked the defenders to surrender, but they had refused, telling him that he would need men with wings in order to capture their impregnable citadel. The 300 volunteers for the assault had gained great experience of rock-climbing during previous sieges in the Central Asian campaign, so were confident in a positive outcome for their mission. Using tent-pegs and strong flaxen lines, they climbed the cliff face at night, losing about thirty men during the ascent. In accordance with their king's orders, they signalled their success to the troops below by waving pieces of linen, at which Alexander sent a herald to shout the news to the enemy's advanced posts and to order them to surrender without further delay. The defenders, surprised and demoralized by the incredible achievement of the party of Macedonian climbers, finally decided to yield. Alexander behaved magnanimously towards the captured Sogdians as he was now seeking a durable peace in Central Asia in order to move out from Sogdia and develop new plans of conquest. For these political and strategic reasons, Alexander married Roxane, the daughter of Oxyartes, thereby cementing a solid alliance with the tribal rulers of the region. The decisive victory at the Sogdian Rock marked the end of Alexander's Central Asian campaign and of his conquest of the Persian Empire.

## Chapter 4

## The Decline of the Scythians

Upon Alexander the Great's death in 323 BC, the Macedonian governor of Thrace was Lysimachus, a general of Thessalian descent who had served for many years under Alexander's direct orders. Under Philip II's rule, Macedonia had conquered Thrace and submitted many of the local tribes, but the region had never been fully pacified. The northern border between Thracian territory and that of the Scythians, marked by the Danube River, soon became an unstable one after Alexander and his Macedonian army left Europe for Asia. The Scythians took advantage of the Macedonians' temporary weakness in the region to launch several devastating incursions across Thrace. The Macedonians responded by organizing a large-scale invasion of Scythia, for which they assembled an army of 30,000 soldiers. These were commanded by Zopyrion, an experienced general who was the governor of Thrace when the expedition was launched in 331 BC. Ancient sources provide very few details of the Macedonian invasion of Scythia, but it is known that the Scythians employed their usual scorched earth strategy to slow down their advancing enemies. The Macedonians were unable to engage the Scythians in a pitched battle as they advanced deeply into southern Ukraine. Zopyrion's objective was to reach the Greek colonies in Ukraine, probably with the intention of annexing them to Macedonia and using their ports for receiving supplies. Once at Olbia Pontica, not far from the Greek cities in Crimea, the Macedonians were surrounded by a massive Scythian army. The ensuing clash was probably the worst military disaster suffered by the Macedonians, with Zopyrion and all 30,000 of his soldiers being massacred by the Scythians. We have no idea how the battle developed, and whether it was an ambush or a pitched clash, but it is reasonable to suppose that the Macedonian phalangites were overcome – on flat terrain – by the superior cavalry of the enemy, with their mounted archers and heavy cavalrymen.

Lysimachus, chosen as the successor of Zopyrion after this catastrophe, faced a very difficult situation in Thrace, where the Macedonian garrison had been reduced to just 4,000 infantrymen and 2,000 cavalry. These were nowhere near sufficient to keep order among the warlike Thracian tribes that were ready to revolt at the first opportunity. Furthermore, the Macedonian presence in the region was not a uniform one: southern Thrace was formally part of the Kingdom of Macedonia, but northern

Scythian dagger. (*Photo and copyright by Amages Drachen*)

Thrace comprised semi-independent tribal kingdoms that were client states of the Macedonians. This meant that the governor of Thrace could exert direct dominance over just one portion of the region. Soon after Lysimachus' arrival, the Odrysians and various other client communities revolted against the Macedonians in the hope of regaining their independence. This Thracian rebellion was particularly violent,

The Decline of the Scythians 73

and Lysimachus had great difficulty in containing it. Vastly outnumbered, he was forced to fight a pitched battle against the Thracians, but against all odds this ended in victory for the Macedonians despite heavy losses. After these events, by 320 BC, the Macedonian general had secured control over Thrace, which he ruled as one of the several independent kingdoms that were created after the collapse of Alexander the Great's empire. Among the various *diadochi* (successor kings), Lysimachus was the one who experienced most difficulty in keeping control over his realm, facing several internal revolts and at the same time being involved in many of the various conflicts that shaped the political map of the Mediterranean after Alexander's death in 323 BC. From the outset, Lysimachus' main political aim was that to conquer Anatolia, wishing to create a large kingdom that could control the Dardanelles and the Bosphorus. To do this, he had to defeat one of the most powerful *diadochi*, Antigonus Monophtalmus, who ruled over a large portion of western Asia that included Anatolia and had strong forces at his command. In 315 BC, Lysimachus joined a military coalition that was established to defeat Antigonus. This comprised the Kingdom of Macedonia ruled by Cassander, the Kingdom of Egypt led by Ptolemy and the Seleucid Empire under the

Scythian warlord. (*Photo and copyright by Scythian State*)

rule of Seleucus. Lysimachus' contribution to this alliance, however, was minimal as he had to face a serious revolt by the northern Thracian tribes that also involved the Scythians, and in addition had to crush a rebellion of the Greek colonies located on the Black Sea coast of Thrace. In 309 BC, Lysimachus built a capital for his Thracian realm, which he named Lysimachia, in a strategic position on the neck connecting Thracian Chersonese with the mainland. Having a capital on the Dardanelles was a clear demonstration of Lysimachus's political ambition, giving him a jumping-off point into Anatolia. In 302 BC a second military coalition against Antigonus was formed, which once again Lysimachus joined, this time more significantly. He entered Anatolia at the head of his army and some allied troops sent by Cassander, but when Antigonus moved against him, Lysimachus opted to retreat and await the arrival of further reinforcements. When these (commanded by Seleucus) reached Anatolia in 301 BC, a decisive battle was fought between Lysimachus and Antigonus at Ipsus. The clash ended in triumph for the allies and resulted in the death of Antigonus. After Ipsus, Lysimachus could finally secure Anatolia, as he had long planned. During the following two decades, he continued fighting against the other *diadochi*, but also tried to expand his domains northwards by crossing the Danube. He launched a major campaign against the Getae, who always resented his rule and could count on the military support of the Scythians. Lysimachus crossed the Danube without meeting opposition but was soon defeated in battle by the Getae and their Scythian allies. He was taken prisoner by the Getae, but was released in 292 BC on the condition that he surrender all the territory he had occupied north of the Danube. In 281 BC, Lysimachus was defeated and killed in battle at Corupedium near Sardis by his *diadochi* rivals, and soon after his death the realm he had created in Thrace collapsed and entered into a state of complete political chaos as the Thracian tribes regained their independence.

While these events took place in the Balkans, the Greek colonies of Ukraine continued to prosper economically thanks to their peaceful co-existence with the Scythians. As we have seen, since 480 BC they were unified into a single Bosporan Kingdom. This confederation of cities had been ruled, since 438 BC, by the Spartocid royal house, which was able to conquer more lands from the Tauri as well as transform the Bosporan Kingdom into a more centralized realm. Satyrus, the successor to the first Spartocid monarch, completed the expansionist process initiated by his predecessor and ruled for a long period (431–387 BC). However, he was unable to capture the city of Theodosia, which had remained independent from the Bosporan Kingdom. This was very significant, as Theodosia was one of the few Greek ports in Crimea that was free from ice throughout the year and thus could continue trading during the winter months. Theodosia was eventually annexed to the Bosporan

Kingdom by Satyrus' son and successor, Leucon, who ruled from 387–347 BC. In 310 BC, following the death of Leucon's heir, Paerisades, a bloody civil war broke out in the Bosporan Kingdom, possession of whose throne was contested by two opposing pretenders, sons of the former king: Satyrus and Eumelus. The civil war fought between the two brothers involved massive participation by the Scythians and an emerging nomadic people, the Sarmatians, who would go on to take the place of the Scythians in southern Ukraine during the following centuries. Satyrus, who was allied with the Scythians, was able to assemble the following troops: 2,000 Greek mercenaries, 2,000 Thracian mercenaries, 20,000 allied Scythian infantrymen and 10,000 allied Scythian cavalrymen. Eumelus, with the support of the Sarmatians, deployed 20,000 cavalry and 22,000 infantry, most of whom were Sarmatians. The decisive battle of the conflict took place at the River Thatis, which was important not only because it determined the destiny of the Bosporan Kingdom but because it was the first occasion where Scythians and Sarmatians fought each other on a large scale.

The work of the historian Diodorus Siculus is the only primary source we have to reconstruct what happened at the Battle of the River Thatis, which was probably located between the lower Kuban River and the Caucasus Mountains, but has never been associated with any of the rivers that actually cross this region. Satyrus deployed his phalanx of 2,000 Greek mercenaries in the centre and his Scythian cavalry on the wings, and began the battle by launching a massive cavalry charge against the centre of the enemy army, which was occupied by the elite heavy cavalry of the Sarmatians. The cavalry clash was won by the Scythians, which convinced Satyrus that he had gained the upper hand. Eumelus, meanwhile, attacked the right wing of his brother's forces and put to flight the Thracian mercenaries. With everything seeming lost for his cause, Satyrus gathered all his Scythian cavalrymen and launched a fresh charge that brought him victory, and caused the complete collapse of Eumelus' forces. Although the Battle of the River Thatis had ended in victory for Satyrus and the Scythians, the civil war for the Bosporan Kingdom was not yet over. Eumelus escaped capture and fled to the lands of the Sarmatians, where he was attacked by his brother. During the ensuing campaign, the Scythians suffered severe casualties and Satyrus was mortally wounded. After the death of his brother, Eumelus finally seized the throne of the Bosporan Kingdom for himself. The century that followed the clash at the River Thatis saw a slow decline of Scythian power and the progressive weakening of the Bosporan Kingdom. The Sarmatians began gaining the upper hand in their confrontation with the Scythians, gradually occupying large parts of the Pontic Steppe (roughly corresponding to southern Russia). By 200 BC, the Scythians had lost control of most of Ukraine and been confined to Crimea by the Sarmatians, who were now much stronger than them militarily. During this last phase of their

Scythian knife. (*Photo and copyright by Amages Drachen*)

# The Decline of the Scythians

long history, the Scythians became more 'hellenized' and started to mix with the Tauri of Crimea, creating a new realm that was strongly linked to the Bosporan Kingdom. Unable to expand their territories towards the Balkans due to the ascendancy of the Sarmatians, the Scythians started to exert increasing pressure over the Greek cities of the Bosporan Kingdom. One of the kingdom's monarchs, Paerisades V, became so hard-pressed by the Scythians that he sought military assistance from a powerful Hellenistic state: the Kingdom of Pontus.

Pontus was founded in 281 BC by Mithridates I, who initiated a Persian dynasty in the north-east of Anatolia by creating a new state. The region of Pontus, located south of the Black Sea on the northern coast of Anatolia, was part of Cappadocia under the Persian Empire and was later conquered by Alexander the Great. The Mithridatic royal house, which ruled Pontus from 281 BC, belonged to the highest level of Persian nobility. Before Alexander the Great, members of this family had been the satraps of Phrygia. The arrival of the Macedonians did not change their situation because they recognized Alexander as their new monarch and thus were able to retain their possessions. In 302 BC, however, Antigonus Monophtalmus invaded Phrygia and killed the ruling Mithridatic satrap, the son of whom

Back view of a Scythian warlord. (*Photo and copyright by Scythian State*)

was able to escape from Phrygia with just a few loyal retainers. After abandoning his homeland, he reached the north-east of Anatolia, where he founded a new independent kingdom by gathering together the areas of northern Cappadocia and eastern Paphlagonia. In 281 BC, the new king assumed the name of Mithridates I and proclaimed the royal dignity of his family. During the following decades, the various monarchs of Pontus fought against the other Anatolian states in order to expand their dominions, the forces of Pontus also launching a series of campaigns against the Greek colonies on the northern coast of Anatolia. The Mithridatic kings, with no access to the Mediterranean, had to find an alternative route for trade and commerce: this alternative was represented by the Black Sea, which soon became the centre of all Pontic economic and political activities. After conquering the Greek cities of the Anatolian coast, Pontic expansionism moved on to Crimea and the western coast of

Scythian warlord. (*Photo and copyright by Scythian State*)

Scythian chieftain. (*Photo and copyright by Scythian State*)

the Caucasus. The Pontic kings started to create very strong political and economic relations with the Greek cities on the northern coast of the Black Sea, as well as with the Greek colonies of the Thracian coast (in the eastern part of modern Bulgaria). As a result of these moves, the Pontic rulers gradually became the masters of the Black Sea.

Initially, the Roman Republic – the new dominant military power of the Mediterranean – did not consider the Kingdom of Pontus as a serious threat because Rome had no interests in the northern part of the Black Sea. This situation changed in 116 BC with the ascendancy to the Pontic throne of Mithridates VI, who had great political ambitions over the whole of Anatolia. Since 150 BC, the Kingdom of Pontus had been gradually 'hellenized' by the Mithridatic monarchs, who abandoned many of their Persian traditions in an attempt to modernize their realm. The results of this process were clearly visible during the reign of Mithridates VI. Differently from the previous kings of Pontus, including his father, he followed a strong anti-Roman agenda from the beginning of his reign. The main political ambition of the new king was to unite the whole Hellenistic world against Rome in order to restore the multinational empire of Alexander the Great. Unlike other Hellenistic monarchs, Mithridates perfectly understood the spirit of Alexander the Great's political vision: the creation of a new multinational state in which peoples with different traditions and cultures could live and prosper in peace. The usual divisions between Macedonians/Greeks and Asian subjects had no sense for the new Pontic king, who was not of Macedonian descent. During the early phase of his reign, Mithridates conquered a large portion of Armenia (located south of the Caucasus) and the strategic Kingdom of Colchis (on the western coast of the Caucasus). The region was rich in many natural resources, including gold, wax, hemp and honey. When the monarch of the Bosporan Kingdom, Paerisades V, asked for help against the Scythians, Mithridates responded by sending his trusted general, Diophantes, to Crimea at the head of a military expedition. The Pontic troops relieved the Greek cities that were under Scythian siege and subdued the Tauri. The Scythians responded to the Pontic intervention by launching an invasion of the Bosporan Kingdom, but this was easily checked by Diophantes, who even established a strong Pontic military base at Eupatorium (on the eastern shore of Crimea). In 107 BC, Mithridates once again sent Diophantes to the Bosporan Kingdom, this time with orders to annex the region. Before this could happen, however, Paerisades V was attacked and killed by the Scythians, who occupied most of Crimea. At this point, Mithridates assembled a large fleet and launched the final Pontic invasion of the Bosporan Kingdom, in which Diophantes defeated the Scythians and annexed the Greek territories in southern Ukraine to the Kingdom of Pontus. Thereafter, the Scythians practically disappeared from history.

Detail of a Scythian sword. (*Photo and copyright by Scythian State*)

Back view of a Scythian chieftain. (*Photo and copyright by Scythian State*)

What remained of their independent territories was conquered by Mithridates, while the Pontic Steppe became the homeland of the Sarmatians. Most of the surviving Scythians were absorbed by the Sarmatians, while others became loyal subjects of Pontus.

In 101 BC, after having secured his empire in the Black Sea region, Mithridates started to expand in Anatolia and invaded the Kingdom of Cappadocia, which was given to his infant son. During the following years, the ambitious Pontic king also formed a strong alliance with the Kingdom of Armenia; the latter was ruled by Tigranes II, who had married Mithridates' daughter, Cleopatra. After these events, the Roman Republic decided that the expansionism of Pontus had to be stopped as soon as possible. The First Mithridatic War broke out in 90 BC when the forces of Pontus invaded the Kingdom of Bithynia and then marched across the Roman province of Asia (the former Kingdom of Pergamon). The local Roman forces were unable to resist, abandoning most of Anatolia to Mithridates. The Pontic invasion was supported by most of the Anatolians, who hated the Romans and their system of heavy taxation. In 88 BC, to present himself as the restorer of Hellenistic freedom, Mithridates ordered the execution of 80,000 Romans living in the province of Asia. In the following months, most of the Greek cities that were formally allied with Rome joined Pontus in the war of liberation against the foreign invaders. With Athens having played a prominent role in this process, a massive Roman army under Sulla besieged the city in 87 BC. Despite the military support of Pontus, Athens was eventually occupied by Sulla. During the following years, the Romans defeated the Pontic aarmy in Greece on two occasions, as a result of which Mithridates was forced to abandon Greece and come to terms with Rome. According to a peace treaty agreed upon in 85 BC, Pontus had to relinquish all the territories that it had occupied in Anatolia: the Kingdom of Cappadocia, the Kingdom of Bithynia and the Roman province of Asia. However, the military capabilities of Mithridates in Asia remained intact. The Second Mithridatic War took place between 83 and 81 BC, but it remained a local conflict that was fought on a small scale between the Roman military forces of Asia and part of Mithridates' army. At the end of the skirmishes that made up this conflict, nothing had changed from territorially. In the following years, the ambitious Pontic monarch started to form new alliances against the Romans, linking up with the pirates of Cilicia and with the Roman usurper Quintus Sertorius (who ruled the Roman territories in Spain, which had temporarily seceded from the central government of the Republic). In 75 BC, the last king of Bithynia died without heirs and left his kingdom to Rome, but two years later Mithridates invaded Bithynia and thereby caused the outbreak of the Third Mithridatic War. This time, the Romans held the military advantage from the beginning. The Pontic army was forced to retreat inside the borders of Pontus, and Mithridates tried in every possible way to avoid a direct confrontation with the Roman legions. In order to achieve his objective, the Pontic king fled to Armenia, where he could count on the support of his ally Tigranes II. During the summer of 69 BC, the Romans invaded Armenia and defeated Tigranes II in a pitched battle fought outside the Armenian capital of Tigranocerta. While the Romans were fighting against the remaining forces of Tigranes II in northern Armenia, Mithridates invaded Pontus again in order to reconquer his kingdom. This time, the Pontic king was able to defeat the Romans in battle, leading to a massive change in the strategic situation of the war. The Roman armies, at risk of being cut off from their lines of supply, had no choice but to abandon Armenia and thus were unable to decisively defeat Tigranes II. The following months were very difficult ones for Rome, Mithridates completing the reconquest of Pontus and the Armenians invading Cappadocia. In 66 BC, however, Pontus and Armenia had to face the enormous Roman military power of Pompey the Great, who had recently crushed the Cilician pirates in the south of Anatolia. Pompey concluded a military alliance with the Parthians of Iran, who attacked Armenia and kept Tigranes II busy in the east. Meanwhile, Pompey marched with all his forces against Pontus. Mithridates was defeated in a major pitched battle and was obliged to flee, going with his few surviving forces to Colchis and then to Crimea. Meanwhile, in 65 BC, Pompey invaded Armenia and defeated Tigranes II. Mithridates was killed during the following months while reorganizing his forces for the defence of Crimea, his death being caused by a revolt of his army which was led by his son, Pharnaces. As a result of these events, the western half of the original Pontic territories were occupied by Rome, while the eastern portion was transformed into a small client kingdom that continued to exist until AD 62. The Crimean possessions of Pontus, now under the guidance of Pharnaces, were reorganized as a newly independent Bosporan Kingdom that was a vassal state of Rome.

The early Pontic army retained military traditions dating back to the Persian period, and thus was largely composed of light troops (both foot and mounted). The original territorial nucleus of Pontus was located in a peripheral zone of the Hellenistic world and had no Macedonian or Greek military settlements inside its borders. Around 150 BC, however, the Pontic monarchs started to transform their army into a Hellenistic force, which was achieved by mixing Macedonian organization and tactics for the infantry with Persian methods for the cavalry. The army of Mithridates VI was always a very multinational force, the ambitious king trying to develop a unified cultural identity among the different peoples living around the Black Sea region in order to unite them against Rome and to bind them to his personal power. In addition to his subjects, Mithridates could also count on several different groups of

Scythian horse archer. (*Photo and copyright by Scythian State*)

mercenaries and allies: Greeks, Thracians, Galatians, Scythians and Sarmatians. All these peoples lived around the Black Sea and provided Pontus with different kinds of troops; Scythians and Sarmatians, of course, mostly provided mounted archers and heavy cavalry. Finding funds to pay the mercenaries was not a problem, while the local levies of Pontic peasants provided strong and resilient recruits who were accustomed to living and fighting on mountainous terrain. From 150 BC, the local Pontic infantrymen started to be equipped and trained as phalangites, abandoning their previous style of fighting based on old Persian models. Under Mithridates VI, the new 'hellenized' contingents of the Pontic army received a proper organization, but it should be remembered that the largest part of Mithridates' forces continued to be composed of Asian light infantry or cavalry. The core of the Pontic infantry was represented by the phalanx, which was organized as an independent division of 15,000 men, its members known as Chalkaspides (bronze shields) and equipped as heavy infantrymen. It is important to note, however, that the quality of Mithridates'

Scythian composite bow and quiver. (*Photo and copyright by Scythian State*)

phalanx was not comparable to that of other Hellenistic armies' phalanxes: Pontic phalangites were peasant levies, not professional soldiers. In order to increase the number of his Chalkaspides in view of the war against Rome, it seems that Mithridates also recruited substantial numbers of freed slaves in his infantry. After defeat in the First Mithridatic War, Mithridates decided to reform his heavy infantry by abandoning the traditional organization based on the phalanx. It is interesting to note that the peace treaty signed with Sulla obliged him to expel all the freed slaves from his forces, so he had to rely on alternative sources of manpower. The total number of the heavy infantrymen was increased from 15,000 to 36,000, and were organized into sixty *cohortes* of 600 soldiers each, following the internal organization of the Roman legions (which were structured on *cohortes*). Of these sixty new units, ten were made up of *thorakitai* (imitation legionaries) and the remaining fifty were of *thureophoroi* (medium infantrymen equipped with oval shields). Apparently, the 6,000 Pontic legionaries were equipped and trained under the guidance of two exiled Roman officers (probably sent by Quintus Sertorius); in addition, they were raised far from Roman eyes, in Crimea and Armenia. Despite all these efforts, the Pontic imitation legionaries proved no match for the 'real' Roman legionaries. The heavy cavalry of Mithridates included an elite squadron of horse companions, formed from the nobility of Pontus and all the personal retainers of the king who came from every corner of Anatolia. We have no precise details about this unit, but we know that its members were equipped as heavy cataphracts. Presumably, the squadron had 400 soldiers like most of the Hellenistic elite cavalry units. The rest of the Pontic heavy cavalry was represented by mercenary and allied cataphracts provided by different peoples: Cappadocians, Armenians, Scythians and Sarmatians. Cataphracts had been introduced into Pontus during the Persian age, but it seems that the best cataphracts under the orders of Mithridates were Cappadocian. Apparently, heavy cavalry was the elite of Mithridates' army and the component that caused most trouble to the Romans. The Pontic cataphracts were usually supplemented by large numbers of scythed chariots, in Persian fashion, but these proved to be of no use against the Roman legions and were progressively abandoned after the end of the First Mithridatic War. Light infantry and light cavalry were both provided by the multinational contingents of allies and mercenaries, which were very numerous but sometimes of little military value. The Greeks from the colonies of northern Anatolia and Crimea mostly served as heavy infantrymen. The Thracians were not extremely numerous and fought in

Scythian horse archer firing with his composite bow. (*Photo and copyright by Scythian State*)

Scythian light cavalryman armed with spear and throwing javelin. (*Photo and copyright by Scythian State*)

their usual manner as light skirmishers, while the Galatians were employed as heavy infantry with large oval shields. The Scythians mostly provided excellent contingents of horse archers, while the Sarmatians could be employed either as cataphracts or mounted archers. Another source of light troops was the Cilician and Cretan pirates, who were allies of Pontus against Rome. Generally speaking, Pontic armies were quite large. In 86 BC, for example, Mithridates deployed the following forces against the Romans: 20,000 Pontic, Cappadocian, Scythian and Sarmatian cavalry, 100,000 infantry (15,000 of whom were Chalkaspides, the rest being light troops) and sixty scythed chariots.

## Chapter 5

## Military Organization and Equipment of the Scythians

The military forces of the Scythians, like those of all the other nomadic peoples of the Eurasian steppes, mostly consisted of cavalry. Indeed, the Scythians were known as the best horse-breeders of the Mediterranean and European world during Antiquity. It is important to note, however, that Scythian armies also included sizeable infantry contingents that were made up of the poorest individuals from each tribal group. Authors like the great Greek historians Herodotus and Thucydides described the Scythian forces as large contingents of mounted archers, while Diodorus Siculus referred to battles that saw the participation of large contingents of Scythian infantry. According to the latest research, it seems that the balance between cavalry and infantry within the Scythian armies changed considerably across the centuries. When the Scythians migrated to the Pontic Steppe, their armies were large cavalry forces; during their early settlement in Ukraine, the Scythians were a people on the move and still had all the distinctive features of the nomadic peoples of Eurasia. They did not have permanent settlements and did not practice agriculture. They moved across the vast plains of the steppe with their horses and cattle, building seasonal camps and following the natural cycles. Over time, as we have seen, the Scythians mixed with the local inhabitants of southern Crimea – the Tauri – and formed new communities that were partially 'hellenized'. As a result, some Scythian groups began building permanent settlements similar to those of the Tauri and started to practice agriculture. It was from these new communities that the large infantry contingents described by Diodorus Siculus came. The early Scythian armies also included foot contingents provided by the sedentary peoples living in Ukraine. These had been transformed into vassals of the nomadic Scythians after the latter had occupied the Pontic Steppe, and as such were required to provide auxiliary contingents. The formidable Scythian cavalry had two main components: horse archers and heavy horsemen. The horse archers were much more numerous than the heavy cavalry, since every able-bodied Scythian male was capable of fighting as a mounted bowman. They wore no armour and were equipped with the deadly composite bow of the Eurasian steppes. While the Scythian commoners made up the light cavalry of the horse archers, the heavy cavalry comprised noble professional warriors who were rich enough to equip themselves with full armour. Broadly speaking, each heavy cavalry contingent was commanded by a prince and consisted of their armed retinue. The professional warriors of the heavy cavalry were used to fight in formation and thus were more disciplined than the horse archers, acting as elite shock troops. Scythian battle tactics were quite simple but worked extremely well in the steppes, having evolved from the movements made by the Scythians while manoeuvring their herds of horses and cattle over the vast plains. These movements had one main objective: concentrating the dispersed animals in a single point of the steppe in order to move them towards new areas of pasture. The battles of the steppe peoples were extremely rapid and violent, beginning with massive attacks by the horse archers, who focused their volleys on the flanks of the enemy in order

Scythian light cavalryman armed with war hammer and throwing javelin. (*Photo and copyright by Scythian State*)

Scythian warrior with his tent in the background. (*Photo and copyright by Amages Drachen*)

to oblige them to concentrate their forces in the centre. When their enemies had been grouped into a single point on the battlefield, the heavily armoured cavalry launched a decisive frontal charge that usually won the day. These tactics worked perfectly against enemies having cavalry armies, but were not always effective when opponents could deploy large heavy infantry contingents (like the Greek hoplites, Macedonian phalangites or Roman legionaries). The Scythian cavalry was famous for its great tactical flexibility: it was capable of regrouping in the thick of the action and of changing direction very rapidly in order to strike where needed. When enemy formations had been broken by the heavy cavalry, the horse archers pursued them in order to transform their retreat into a rout. In many aspects the Scythians were a 'people at arms', since each Scythian male had the necessary personal equipment and expertise to be a soldier. Even the poorest individuals, who did not own a horse, contributed to the war efforts of their community by fighting as lightly equipped foot skirmishers, mostly armed with throwing javelins.

Scythian dead were buried in barrow-mounds known as kurgans, each Scythian warrior accompanied on his journey into eternity by the possessions that were most important to him in life. These, of course, included his weapons, so thanks to the rich finds of military equipment that have emerged from excavations of Scythian barrows, it is possible to build a very clear picture of what Scythian armour and offensive weapons looked like. The grave of a common warrior, who had fought as a horse archer, usually contained just a few elements: a composite bow, several dozen arrows and a couple of spears. The tombs of nobles and kings, however, included whole arsenals of top-quality weapons, with armour, helmets, swords, quivers full of arrows, dozens of spears and horse skeletons with full military harness. The standard kind of armour worn by most of the Scythian warriors consisted of flexible leather corselets that were partly or entirely covered with overlapping scales of bronze or iron. The Scythians were masters in producing bronze scale armour, and did not cover only leather corselets with metal scales; their helmets and shields were also frequently reinforced by applying bronze or iron scales on their external surface. Scythian armourers cut the scales from sheet metal with a pointed tool or with shears, and the scales were then attached to the soft leather base of the corselets by thin leather thongs or animal tendons. Each individual scale was set in such a way that it covered between a third and half of the width of the next scale sideways. Each single row of scales overlapped the one placed below it, protecting the stitching where it was exposed in holes through the metal. Despite providing excellent protection to their wearers, the corselets did not significantly hinder the movement of a mounted warrior. Various types of corselets were used, according to the economic capabilities of their wearers. The simplest and cheapest ones had metal scales only around the neck and upper breast, or only on the front surface. Short-sleeved corselets were used by the common warriors, while the nobility could often have long-sleeved versions. Quite frequently, a doubled yoke of scale-work was applied across the upper back and extended forward over the shoulders to the sides of the breast, in order to offer better protection for the shoulders. The scales of a single corselet could sometimes be made from two different materials, in order to look even more magnificent, polished bronze scales glittering in the sun against the lustreless iron scales. Scythian kings and princes could have corselets entirely covered with golden scales.

The early helmets of the Scythians were of the Kuban type, heavy cast-bronze helmets that fitted tightly to the skull and protected it way down the face by means of cheek-pieces that left cut-outs for the eyes. From the fifth century BC onwards, the Kuban helmet started to be replaced by the new Phrygian type, a forward-pointing Phrygian cap made of leather and covered with metal scales. The Phrygian cap was extremely popular in the Balkans and was worn by most of the Thracian tribes, so it is highly probable that the Scythians started wearing it after coming into contact with them. Phrygian helmets could have cheek-pieces and neck-guards, always made of leather covered with metal scales. Being easy and cheap to produce, the Phrygian helmets were also used also by the majority of the Scythian common warriors. With the progression of time, Scythian noblemen started to purchase increasing numbers of bronze helmets from the merchants of the Greek colonies in Crimea. These, according to recent findings, were mostly worn by the Scythian heavy cavalry and could be of the following Hellenic models: Corinthian, Chalcidian or Attic. The defensive equipment of a Scythian noble warrior often included leg guards, which could be made of leather covered with scales or might consist of bronze greaves purchased in the Greek colonies of Crimea. Leggings covered with bronze or iron

Scythian light cavalryman armed with spear and throwing javelin. (*Photo and copyright by Scythian State*)

Detail of a Scythian dagger. (*Photo and copyright by Amages Drachen*)

scales were a distinctive element of the Scythian heavy cavalry's panoply. The Greek-style bronze greaves of the richest individuals could be gilded and have decorative incisions. Both the helmets and greaves purchased from the Greek merchants were part of the hoplites' heavy infantry equipment, the Scythians adapting them to their traditional defensive panoply.

The poorest Scythian warriors, fighting as light horsemen or light infantry, had simple shields made from woven osiers, whereas noble fighters employed massive shields faced with iron. The latter were constructed from a wooden base that was covered with scales of iron, which were sewn to each other and to the backing with wire. Sometimes, kings and princes could have shields covered with a single iron plate, being decorated with applied motifs made from other metals. Deer and panthers were the wild animals most frequently represented in Scythian decorations. Scythian shields were usually rectangular with curved angles, but could sometimes be crescent-shaped like those of the Thracians. The poorest Scythian warriors, especially those serving as light infantrymen, wore only a girdle for protection of their body. This was made of leather covered with metal scales, being broad enough to cover the whole abdomen. Armour worn by the horses of the Scythian heavy cavalry evolved considerably across the centuries. Initially, it consisted just of metal plates and pendant decorations attached to the bridle for protection of the horse's head, but over time pieces of leather horse-cloth covered with metal scales were introduced and became increasingly popular. A thick felt apron for the horse's breast was also developed, in order to provide better protection against enemy arrows. The Scythians, like all the other steppe peoples of Antiquity, rode without stirrups but were masters in the production of bridles, which were often decorated with bronze disks or plates. Scythian saddles were quite flat and simple, being made from leather.

Every Scythian man had a composite bow and arrows, the bow being the national weapon of the Scythian and all the nomadic warriors of the steppes. Contemporary written sources describe the Scythian composite bows as being unstrung and recurved, their overall shape resembling that of the Greek letter *sigma* or a crescent moon with both ends curved inwards. The Scythian bow was quite short – just 80cm – but extremely powerful thanks to its composite construction. The composite bow was made from horn, wood and sinew laminated together. The horn was on the belly facing the archer, while sinew was on the outer side of the wooden core. The wooden core gave the bow its shape and dimensional stability. When the bow was drawn, the sinew (stretched on the outside) and horn (compressed on the inside) stored more energy than the wood for the same length of bow. The construction of a composite bow was a very complex process, requiring more varieties of material than a wooden bow and much more time. It was often made of multiple pieces, joined

Thracian chieftain. (*Photo and copyright by Ancient Thrace*)

Thracian light infantryman. (*Photo and copyright by Ancient Thrace*)

with animal glue in V-shaped splices. Pieced construction allowed the use of woods with different mechanical properties for the bending and non-bending sections, the wood of the bending part of the limb having to endure intense shearing stress. A thin layer of horn was glued onto what would be the belly of the bow; this could store more energy than wood in compression. Goat and sheep horn was commonly used for this purpose. The sinew, soaked in animal glue, was then laid in layers on the back of the bow, the strands of sinew being oriented along the weapon's length. The sinew was normally obtained from the lower legs and back of wild deer or domestic ungulates. Sinew would extend further than wood, again allowing more energy storage. Hide glue was used to attach layers of sinew to the back of the bow and to fix the horn belly to the wooden core. The animal glue could lose strength in humid conditions and be quickly ruined by submersion or rain, so composite bows were always stored in protective leather cases. Historically, peoples living in humid or rainy regions have favoured wooden bows, while those inhabiting dry or arid lands have preferred composite ones. The main advantage of composite bows over longbows was their combination of smaller size with high power. In addition, composite bows are recurved, as their shape curves away from the archer, this design giving them higher draw-weight in the early stages of the archer's draw, thus storing more total energy. The string of the Scythian bows was made from horsehair or animal tendon. Each bow was carried in a special case slung from the waistbelt, made of leather. The case, called the *gorytos*, was often covered with metal plates on the external surface and could contain up to seventy-five arrows. As a result, it worked both as a case for the bow and as a quiver for the arrows. The shaft of an arrow was made from reed or a thin birch branch, while the fletching was made from birds' feathers. The heads of the arrows were of bronze or iron and had different shapes according to the use that the archer had to make of them. Standard arrows used for fighting had trilobate heads that were capable of piercing enemy armour from long distances thanks to their excellent aerodynamic form. Skilled Scythian archers were capable of firing between ten and twelve arrows in a minute and could hit a target at a distance of some 500m.

The earliest Scythian swords derived from those used by the Cimmerians, with a two-edged and almost parallel-sided blade tapering at the point. The blade was 60–70cm long. Daggers, having the same basic features and being employed as secondary weapons, had blades 35–40cm long. Early Scythian swords were decorated with thin gold plates fixed round the hilt. Over time, Scythian swords changed the shape of their blades, which became that of an elongated isosceles triangle with a continuous taper down its whole length. During the fourth century BC, single-edged versions of this new kind of blade started to be produced. The pommel of Scythian swords, which had a simple crossbar shape in the early types, gradually changed to be more

Thracian warrior. (*Photo and copyright by Ancient Thrace*)

# Military Organization and Equipment of the Scythians 101

Thracian sword and knife. (*Photo and copyright by Ancient Thrace*)

complex, with two talons of iron rising and curling inwards. The grip, initially having a cylindrical shape, gradually came to be double-tapered or oval, which was more practical for use in combat. The guard evolved to have a triangular shape, with a sharp and curved indent in the centre of its bottom edge. The scabbards of Scythian swords were made of wood covered with leather and hung from the waistbelt by a thong passing through its projecting ear. Swords had a very important religious function among the Scythians, who frequently built ceremonial altars in the steppe that had a single sacred sword placed on top of them. As a result, they were a noble weapon that was passed from father to son.

Scythian horsemen used different kinds of spears, according to the tactical function that they had to perform on the battlefield. Heavy cavalrymen were equipped with long spears of the *kontus* type. These were about 4m long and had to be wielded with two hands while directing the horse using the knees; it was a specialist weapon that required a lot of training and good horsemanship to use. The *kontus* was reputedly a weapon of great power compared to other cavalry spears of the time. The great length of this deadly weapon was probably the origin of its name, since the Greek word *kontus* means 'oar' or 'barge-pole'. The heavy cavalrymen who formed the personal retinue of a Scythian prince and wore full armour were usually armed with the *kontus*, which was employed as a shock weapon during frontal charges. Shorter spears, about

Points of Thracian spear and javelins. (*Photo and copyright by Ancient Thrace*)

1.7–1.8m long, were used for throwing and thrusting by both Scythian cavalry and infantry. These weapons had leaf-shaped heads with a central spine, as well as a socket for the wooden shaft. Scythian light cavalrymen and light infantrymen carried throwing javelins instead of the spears described above. These had a long iron shank with a small pyramidal head, which was sharply barbed and was designed to pierce enemy shields. The Scythians, in addition to swords, also employed other weapons for hand-to-hand fighting, including battleaxes and maces. Axes had iron blades that could be richly decorated, while maces had lobbed heads and were also used as symbols of authority.

## Chapter 6

## The Early History of the Sarmatians

The origins of the Sarmatians are controversial, exactly like those of the Scythians, since no written primary sources created by the same Sarmatians exist. What we do know for sure, however, is that the early Sarmatian culture had a lot in common with that of the Saka (called Eastern Scythians or Asiatic Scythians by several contemporary Greek historians). The Sarmatians comprised several different tribes, and if compared with the Scythians were more fragmented politically. The earliest Sarmatian community recorded in the work of Greek authors is that of the Sauromates, who probably gave their name to all the Sarmatian peoples. The Sauromates lived on the eastern bank of the Don River in the sixth century BC and were strongly linked to the Scythians, speaking a corrupted form of the Scythian language. When the Persian monarch Darius I attacked Scythia in 513 BC, the Sauromates joined forces with the Scythians and sent military contingents to Ukraine in order to fight against the Achaemenid troops. By the end of the fifth century BC, the Sauromates had disappeared from history, probably being absorbed by the Scythians or contributing to the formation of the later Sarmatian groups. During the last decades of the fifth century BC, a new Sarmatian tribe, the Siraces, migrated from present-day Kazakhstan to the Don River region of southern Russia. The Siraces established their homeland north of Scythia but gradually expelled the Scythians from the interior areas of the Caucasus. Here, they met for the first time the Greeks living in the colonies of the Black Sea, with whom they established commercial relations. During the civil war that ravaged the Bosporan Kingdom in 310 and 309 BC, the Sarmatian Siraces sided with Eumelos and provided him with sizeable military contingents. As we have seen, the Siraces were defeated by the Scythians at the Battle of the River Thatis, but were later able to emerge as a significant military power of the Pontic Steppe. North of the territories inhabited by the Siraces were the Aorsi, another Sarmatian group. These were not a single group but a confederation of tribes, as a result of which they were much more numerous than the Siraces. The homeland of the Aorsi corresponded to a large portion of present-day southern Russia. Both the Siraces and the Aorsi became involved in the politics of the Bosporan Kingdom, which was a vassal state of the Roman Republic after the fall of Pontus. In 48 BC, the ruling monarch of Crimea, Pharnaces II, decided

Sarmatian heavy cavalryman. (*Photo and copyright by Amages Drachen*)

to play a role in the ongoing Roman civil war that had the supporters of Caesar and Pompey fighting against each other. The Bosporan Kingdom supported Pompey and landed an expeditionary force on the northern coastline of Anatolia. The military forces of Pharnaces II were able to obtain a clear victory over the local Roman troops, which were pro-Caesar. As a result, for a short time, it seemed that the Bosporan Kingdom would occupy Pontus. Julius Caesar, however, responded very rapidly to the actions of Pharnaces II, landing in Anatolia at the head of a small military force. He advanced against the 20,000 Bosporan soldiers and defeated them at the Battle of Zela, Caesar's campaign being so rapid (just five days) that to commemorate it the great Roman general invented the famous expression '*Veni, vidi, vici*' ('I came, I saw, I conquered'). Following the defeat at Zela, Pharnaces and his troops returned to the Bosporan Kingdom, where the monarch had to face a revolt led by his son-in-law, Asander, who killed Pharnaces and took the throne for himself. Caesar, meanwhile, chose Mithridates of Pergamum (one of his Anatolian allies) as the new ruler of the Bosporan Kingdom. As a result of these events, a civil war broke out in Ukraine between Asander and Mithridates. The Sarmatians were heavily involved in this conflict, the more 'hellenized' Siraces supporting Asander while the Aorsi sided with the pro-Roman Mithridates. Eventually, Mithridates prevailed in the internecine war, mostly thanks to the support of Julius Caesar. Following Octavian's rise as the first emperor of Rome some years later, however, Mithridates was removed as monarch of the Bosporan Kingdom and replaced by the Romans with Asander, who ruled as a loyal client king of Augustus until his death in 17 BC. Following the Bosporan civil war of 49 BC, both the Siraces and the Aorsi lost most of their previous importance: the former almost disappeared from history after having been submitted by the Romans, while the latter were absorbed by another Sarmatian group, the Alani.

Around 120 BC, another two Sarmatian tribes – the Iazyges and Roxolani – started to be mentioned in the contemporary written sources compiled by Greek or Roman authors. These roamed across southern Ukraine, defeating the Scythians on several occasions due to their superior numbers. The Iazyges and Roxolani came from the heart of the Eurasian steppes, and thus looked much more 'barbarian' than the Scythians to the contemporary Greek and Roman observers. In 107 BC, they temporarily joined forces with the Scythians to fight against the Pontic troops of Diophantes, but were soundly defeated in battle by them. According to Strabo, Diophantes, with just 6,000 well-trained Pontic infantrymen, was able to rout a Sarmatian army of 50,000 warriors. After this defeat, many of the Iazyges and Roxolani entered the ranks of the Pontic army as auxiliaries or mercenaries, thereafter participating in the wars fought by the Kingdom of Pontus against the Roman Republic. After the fall of Pontus, the Sarmatians moved westwards across Crimea and established themselves north of the Danube, where they started to launch some minor incursions against the Balkan territories of Rome that were located south of the great river and came into contact with the Dacians. The Iazyges established their homeland in modern Hungary, between the Danube and Tisza rivers, whereas the Roxolani settled north of the lower Danube. From the early decades of the first century AD, the history of both Sarmatian tribes became strongly linked with that of the Dacians.

During the fourth century BC, while the Celts from Gaul were expanding towards the British Isles and Spain, those from Austria and western Hungary started to move across Eastern Europe. The main driving force of Celtic expansionism in that part of the continent was represented, at least initially, by the two large groups of the Boii and Volcae. These were not simple tribes, but confederations made up of several smaller tribal communities. Moving from Austria, the Celts completed their conquest of Hungary and advanced also along the Danube in order to occupy large territories in the Carpathian region. By the end of the fourth century BC, the Celtic presence in present-day Slovakia, the Czech Republic, Hungary and south-western Poland was quite stable, but the Celts then decided to move further south and east, following two different routes. The first route crossed the territories of modern Slovenia and Croatia, in the northern part of the western Balkans, where the Celtic tribes had to face the Illyrians, who tried to resist with all their resources despite being outnumbered by the northern invaders. The second route followed the Danube and was directed to the Black Sea, running across Transylvania (the western part of modern Romania) and reaching the western part of present-day Ukraine. At that time, present-day Romania had already seen the emergence of the Dacian culture, which had many aspects in common with the Thracian one but was completely separate from the latter. The Celtic presence in Dacia soon became quite significant, but the newcomers always had to co-exist with the local population, as the Scythians had done before them. This situation continued until 150 BC, when the Dacians started to fight against the Celtic communities living on their territories with the aim of expelling them from Transylvania. This was not a simple process, because the Celts had firmly established themselves in Dacia. The Dacians, however, were supported in their long struggle by the powerful Thracian tribe of the Getae, who controlled a portion of territory north of the Danube. The violent conflict between Dacians and Celts came to a critical point around 60 BC, when Burebista emerged as a great war leader from the tribes of Dacia. Burebista guided the Dacians in the decisive moment of the conflict against the Celts and expelled them from the middle Danube region. Soon after achieving his objectives, Burebista was crowned as overlord of the Dacians and started to unify all the tribes of his people into some sort of centralized state. This developed quite rapidly thanks to the skill of Burebista, who ordered the construction of a system of hill forts across Dacia in order to control the territories of the various communities and gradually absorbed the powerful Getae inside his political sphere of influence. Until 40 BC, he continued to fight on the borders of his new state against the Boii, who still represented a potential threat for Dacia and continued to launch raids against Burebista's lands. During this period, however, the Dacians were also at war with another two peoples: the Bastarnae and the Scordisci.

The Bastarnae were a large tribe of mixed Celtic-Germanic descent, which originally settled in present-day Moldavia before moving south towards the heart of the Balkans around 200 BC. In 179 BC the Bastarnae crossed the Danube in great numbers, having been invited to do so by Philip V of Macedonia. King Philip had recently been defeated by the Romans during the Second Macedonian War and had been obliged by the victors to drastically reduce the size of his armed forces. This caused serious problems to Macedonia, the new army being too small to effectively defend the eastern borders of the realm from the regular attacks by Illyrian and Thracian tribes. To resolve this issue, Philip V intended to settle the Bastarnae on his eastern frontier as military colonists, so they would defend the area from enemy raids and be loyal subjects of the Macedonians. Furthermore, in case of a new war against Rome – which was very probable – they could be employed as a significant part of the Macedonian army. The Bastarnae accepted Philip V's offer and started to migrate south, but while on the march they learned that the Macedonian king had died and they were no longer expected in their new homeland. At this point, having reached Thrace, they decided to raid and pillage the region. Hostilities between the Bastarnae and the Thracians were particularly violent, the former besieging various Thracian strongholds but without success and later being ambushed on several occasions by Thracian warriors. Half of the Bastarnae then decided to return north to their homeland, while the remainder – some 30,000 people – remained on the eastern frontier of Macedonia. Philip V's successor, Perseus, allowed the Bastarnae to settle on the territory of the Illyrian and Thracian tribes that attacked the eastern Macedonian frontier. These tribes assaulted the winter camp that had been built by the Bastarnae but were repulsed with heavy losses. The conflict continued with an offensive by the Bastarnae against their enemies, but the Celtic-Germanic warriors were crushed in an ambush. The Bastarnae, having little knowledge of their new homeland, were greatly exposed to ambushes when moving in great numbers, but during pitched battles they were superior to any enemy. Having lost their entire baggage and supplies during the ambush, they had no choice but to return home to Moldavia. Many of them died while crossing the frozen Danube on foot, and others were killed by the local tribes. Some decades after these events, the Bastarnae were gradually able to recover from the losses suffered during their failed migration,

Detail of a Sarmatian sword. (*Photo and copyright by Amages Drachen*)

Detail of a Sarmatian quiver and dagger. (*Photo and copyright by Amages Drachen*)

but they then found themselves at war with the expanding Dacian Kingdom of Burebista. The Dacian monarch wanted to unify all the peoples living along the eastern part of the Danube under his personal rule and had in mind to attack the Romans in Macedonia to expel them from the region. To do this, he sought to secure the decisive military support of the Bastarnae, who were considered the best warriors of the Balkans by most contemporary observers. Hostilities between the Dacians and the Bastarnae did not last for long, resulting in victory for Burebista. The Celtic-Germanic warriors then became allies of the Dacians and contributed to the further enlargement of Burebista's army.

The Scordisci, a Celtic tribe originally settled in modern Hungary, had participated in the great Celtic invasion of the Balkans. During their march home from a raiding expedition, the Scordisci decided to stop at the mouth of the River Sava and to build new settlements there. Philip V of Macedonia developed a very good relationship with them, wanting to use the Celts as allies against the Illyrian and Thracian tribes and Rome (exactly like he did with the Bastarnae). The Scordisci soon became a significant regional power in the central Balkans, constructing two fortresses to protect their new territory and submitting several of the local tribes, including the Paeonians. After the transformation of Macedonia into a Roman province in 146 BC, the Scordisci were constantly at war against the Romans, launching frequent incursions against their territory. In 135 BC, Rome obtained its first victory over the Scordisci, but in 114 BC an entire Roman expeditionary force (commanded by Gaius Porcius Cato) was destroyed by Celtic tribesmen. Another two campaigns followed in 112 and 107 BC, but the Romans were unable to expel the Celts from the mountains of present-day western Serbia. In 88 BC, the Roman Republic organized a major military expedition against the Scordisci, who had pillaged as far as Delphi in Greece during the previous years. This time the Romans obtained a decisive victory and the power of the Scordisci was definitively crushed. They had no choice but to move north of the Danube in search of new lands to settle upon. Between 55 and 50 BC they found themselves at war with the Dacian Kingdom of Burebista, who wanted to transform them into his subjects or allies. The Dacians eventually emerged victorious from this conflict, and the Scordisci – like the Getae and the Bastarnae – came under the political influence of Burebista. The Dacian ruler, after having secured control over most of the eastern Balkans, started to make aggressive moves towards Roman Macedonia and launched several raids against the Illyrian and Thracian tribes living on his southern borders. From 55 BC, the Dacians also started to attack the Greek colonies located on the Black Sea coastline. These were conquered one by one, which the Thracians had never been able to do. The Romans did very little to counter Dacian expansionism during this phase, being heavily involved on other fronts.

Sarmatian horse archer. (*Photo and copyright by Amages Drachen*)

Detail of a Sarmatian knife. (*Photo and copyright by Amages Drachen*)

Julius Caesar was completing the conquest of Gaul, and the possibility of a civil war between him and Pompey was becoming more likely. That internecine conflict duly erupted in 49 BC and affected the whole Mediterranean, each state bordering with the Roman Republic being forced to take a position in favour of Caesar or Pompey. Burebista chose to support Pompey, but the Roman general was defeated and killed before he could send any troops to Roman Macedonia. Caesar, well aware of the Dacians' military potential, considered Burebista a dangerous enemy. Indeed, after becoming the sole ruler of Rome Caesar started planning a punitive expedition against Dacia, but he was assassinated before the campaign could be launched. Some months after Julius Caesar's death, Burebista was also killed as the result of a plot organized by the Dacian aristocracy, which resented the new centralized form of government introduced by Burebista and feared the possibility of an armed conflict with Rome. Soon after these events, the Dacian Kingdom temporarily collapsed and was broken up into several smaller realms that quickly started to quarrel between themselves. All the great political achievements of Burebista were lost and a new phase in the history of the Dacians began.

Sarmatian horse archer. (*Photo and copyright by Amages Drachen*)

# The Early History of the Sarmatians 115

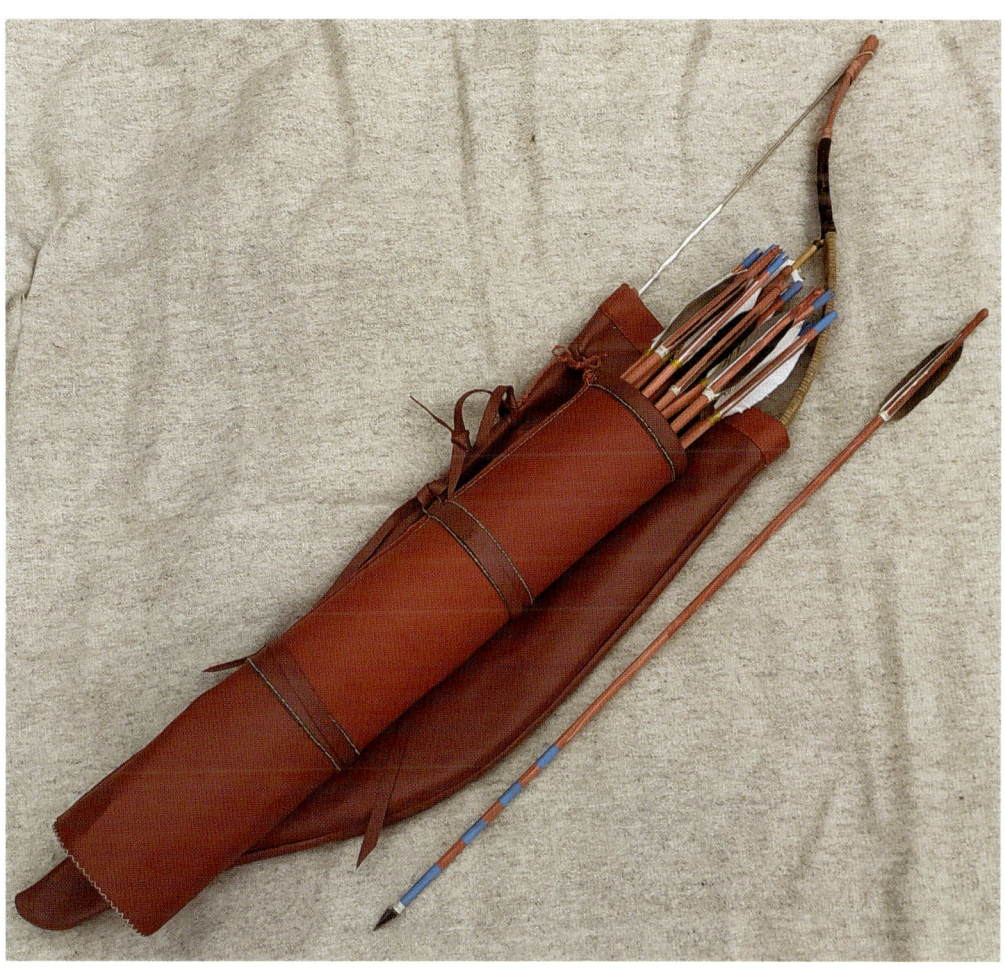

Sarmatian composite bow and quiver. (*Photo and copyright by Amages Drachen*)

## Chapter 7

## The Sarmatians and the Dacian Wars

Following Burebista's death, the Dacians no longer represented a threat for the Romans. Their large kingdom was fragmented into several parts and the great multi-national army created by Burebista – numbering around 100,000 warriors – no longer existed. The Roman Republic abandoned Caesar's plans for an invasion of Dacia and limited itself to keeping order on the Balkan frontier. This situation started to change only in AD 69, when a new Dacian leader, named Duras, emerged. Until the end of Augustus' reign (AD 14), Dacia continued to be divided into five smaller kingdoms that could all be easily controlled by the Romans. In the following decades, however, a new sense of national identity started to emerge among the Dacian communities. Rome was increasingly perceived as a deadly menace, with all the Dacians feeling the need for joint action against the Mediterranean powerhouse. Duras became king in AD 69 after his father, Scorilo, was killed during a Dacian raid against the Roman province of Moesia that saw the participation of the Roxolani as allies of the Dacians. Moesia had become a province during Augustus' reign as a buffer zone between Macedonia and Dacia, being located to the north of Macedonia and south-west of Dacia. Before the Romans' arrival, this region was inhabited by the Moesi (a tribe of Dacian stock), the Triballi (a Thracian tribe) and some of the Bastarnae. The Romans considered Moesia a key region and thus decided to conquer it in order to protect Macedonia from incursions by the barbarians north of the Danube. The northern border of the new province was marked by the course of the great river. The *casus belli* for the invasion of Moesia was provided to the Romans by the Bastarnae, who attacked one of their allied Thracian tribes. During the ensuing conflict, thousands of Bastarnae were killed by the Romans and the Moesi were forced to submit. Before more reinforcements sent by the northern Bastarnae could move south of the Danube, the Romans completed the conquest of Moesia, which was transformed into one of their provinces in AD 6. The Dacians never accepted Rome's conquest of Moesia and soon started to attack the region. An incursion headed by Scorilo in AD 69 was the first major attack, but ended in failure.

After Scorilo's death, Duras became king and continued the policy of his predecessor. He started to rebuild the military power of the Dacians and strove to reunify the various tribes of his people. In AD 85, Duras assembled a large army and

# The Sarmatians and the Dacian Wars

Sarmatian light cavalryman using his lasso. (*Photo and copyright by Amages Drachen*)

Detail of a Sarmatian knife. (*Photo and copyright by Amages Drachen*)

invaded Moesia from the north, the attack being a great success with the Romans unable to halt the marauding Dacians. An entire legion was annihilated by the joint forces of the Dacians and the Roxolani, and the governor of Moesia, Oppius Sabinus, was killed during the major battle of this campaign. It became clear in Rome that something had changed in Dacia: there was now a strong enemy leader along that sector of the frontier who had the necessary military resources to occupy Moesia. Emperor Domitian acted swiftly to repulse Duras' offensive, travelling to Moesia at the head of a large force and moved three legions to the territory of the menaced province. When the Roman army arrived, however, the Dacians avoided a direct confrontation with the superior forces of their enemy. The war continued for several months, but without any major change in the strategic situation. On one occasion, the Romans were ambushed and defeated by the Dacians, but the latter also suffered several defeats. In AD 86/87, Duras abdicated in favour of a younger Dacian war leader named Decebalus, who had been the main military commander of the Dacians from the beginning of the conflict with Rome and had shown great personal abilities on several occasions. The new king quickly understood that there was no point in continuing the war with Rome, at least for the moment, since the Roman garrison of

Moesia was by now too strong to be defeated. As a result, after Emperor Domitian had already left the theatre of operations, a peace treaty was concluded between the Dacians and the Roman Empire. Decebalus had to return the many Roman prisoners who had been captured by the Dacians and promise not to attack Moesia in the future, in exchange for which he obtained Rome's military assistance to build new fortifications in his kingdom and an annual subsidy of 8 million sesterces.

Thanks to the new fortifications that were built with the help of the Romans, Decebalus was able to complete the reunification of Dacia that had been initiated by his predecessor and transform his realm into a centralized state. With the large amounts of money sent every year by the Romans, he could also enlarge and re-equip his armies, transforming them into a very efficient combat machine. Decebalus soon proved to be an excellent king, not only from a military point of view but also economically and administratively. He started to exploit in a methodical way all the great mineral resources of his kingdom in order to produce larger amounts of precious metals, and also reorganized the structures of his state in order to exert better control over the peripheral areas of Dacia, where the local tribes were all brought under his influence. Decebalus also ordered the creation of a fortified capital for his realm, known as Sarmizegetusa. The new city soon became the most important political and religious centre of Dacia, being established on top of a mountain, at an altitude of 1,200m, in the centre of the Dacian Kingdom. Sarmizegetusa, thanks to its position and strong walls, was extremely easy to defend, comprising six connected citadels and being part of a larger system of fortifications. Sarmizegetusa had already functioned as the capital of the Dacians during the reign of Burebista, but after his death it had lost its special status. Up until the rise of Decebalus, it had never been fortified or enlarged. During the decade that followed the end of hostilities between Dacia and Rome, Decebalus transformed his kingdom into one of the most flourishing states of Antiquity. He controlled a large area of European territory, corresponding to modern Romania, and could put in the field an impressive army of over 200,000 warriors. The Romans soon realized that signing a peace treaty with the Dacians had been a mistake, particularly as the conditions offered to Decebalus had been so positive. Sooner or later, it was felt, the Dacians would attack Moesia again, and the Empire had to be ready to react. The Romans had bad memories of their previous war with the Dacians, the defeat of Oppius Sabinus and the humiliation suffered by the legions having not been forgotten. Decebalus had been responsible for that Roman failure when he was still a military commander: at that time he was known as Diurpaneus, since he only received the new name of Decebalus (i.e. 'the Brave') after defeating and killing Oppius Sabinus in what became known as the First Battle of Tapae.

Sarmatian horse archer. (*Photo and copyright by Historia Renascita*)

Sarmatian knife. (*Photo and copyright by Amages Drachen*)

In AD 97, Trajan became Emperor of Rome and started to deal with the most important military issues of his state. He considered Dacia a substantial threat for the stability of the Empire, since it was too large to be considered a normal client state of Rome. In AD 101, after obtaining the Senate's official blessing, Trajan started his preparations for the invasion of Dacia. By conquering Dacia, the Romans would stabilize once and for all their northern borders on the Danube and would also obtain access to the vast natural resources of a region that had never been fully explored. From a cultural point of view, Dacia was a kingdom located on the edge of the known world. Indeed, the Romans had little knowledge of the region, considering the Dacians as merely one of the many barbarian peoples living on their frontiers. Nevertheless, Trajan prepared his invasion with great attention and assembled a large military force to conduct it. The Dacians also made detailed preparations, under the intelligent guidance of Decebalus. The king made particular efforts to conclude an important military alliance with the Sarmatians. Decebalus was able to establish a solid pact with the powerful tribe of the Roxolani, who provided him with large contingents of top-quality cavalry, although the Iazyges preferred to remain neutral in the hope of receiving some lands of the Roxolani in the event of a Roman victory. Trajan reached the province of Moesia in the spring of AD 101 at the head of one of the largest armies ever assembled in the long history of Rome, comprising no less than fifteen legions, ten *vexillationes* (i.e. detachments) of legions and eighty-nine corps of auxiliaries. The legions were the *I Adiutrix*, *I Italica*, *I Minervia*, *II Adiutrix*,

*II Traiana Fortis*, *III Flavia*, *V Macedonica*, *VII Claudia*, *X Gemina*, *XI Claudia Pia Fidelis*, *XIII Gemina*, *XIV Gemina Martia Victrix*, *XV Apollinaris*, *XXI Rapax* and *XXX Ulpia Victrix*. The *vexillationes* came from the following legions: *II Augusta*, *III Augusta*, *III Gallica*, *IV Scythica*, *VI Ferrata*, *VII Gemina*, *IX Hispana*, *XII Fulminata*, *XX Valeria Victrix* and *XXII Primigenia*. The corps of *auxilia* comprised twenty-one *alae* of cavalry, thirty-three *cohortes equitatae* (mixed infantry and cavalry units), twenty-five *cohortes peditatae* (infantry) and ten *cohortes sagittariae* (archers). In total, Trajan could count on 75,000 legionaries and 55,000 auxiliaries, these being supplemented by another 20,000 *auxilia* soldiers who were transferred to Moesia specifically for this campaign (the other 55,000 were already stationed along the Danube before the outbreak of hostilities). The emperor also brought with him the famous Praetorian Guard, which was the elite of the Roman army and comprised Trajan's mounted escort. The Roman invasion force was divided into two large columns, which crossed the Danube on two pontoon bridges that were built with the warships of the Roman river fleet. Trajan's war plan was simple: he wanted to cross southern Dacia as soon as possible, ravaging all the enemy settlements encountered along the way, in order to rapidly reach the Iron Gates, a narrow mountain pass west of the Dacian capital. Capturing the Iron Gates was the only way to approach Sarmizegetusa and to enter the main fortified system of the Dacians. During the first phase of the campaign, Decebalus acted very intelligently, avoiding direct confrontation with the Romans and employing scorched earth tactics. All the food reserves of southern Dacia were moved north or destroyed before the Romans could capture them, the Dacians retreating towards the heart of their territory and obliging the Romans to move across densely forested areas. The Romans knew very little of these interior regions, and as they moved forward their supply lines became increasingly stretched, to the point of being dangerously exposed to Dacian incursions.

Trajan continued his advance very slowly, in order to avoid possible ambushes and to consolidate his presence on Dacian territory. While moving north, the Romans built camps, roads and bridges, meaning they would have been able to put up a strong resistance in southern Dacia in case of defeat. When the Romans reached the Iron Gates, Decebalus decided that the time had finally come to fight a pitched battle. What became known as the Second Battle of Tapae was extremely hard-fought by both sides. The Romans were eventually able to repulse the Dacian assaults, but only after suffering severe losses. Decebalus lost many warriors too, but he had the time and resources to replace them. At this point of the conflict, the Dacians retreated behind the Iron Gates and inside their main fortified system, while the Romans built a massive winter camp not far from the entrance to the mountain pass. During the early months of AD 102, with the Roman army blocked outside the

Germanic warrior of the Bastarnae, armed with spear. (*Photo and copyright by Ancient Thrace*)

Germanic warrior of the Bastarnae, armed with club. (*Photo and copyright by Ancient Thrace*)

Iron Gates, Decebalus decided to act on another front to divert Trajan's attention. Together with his Roxolani allies, he attacked Moesia from the north at the head of a massive force. The Roman garrison of Moesia had great difficulties in containing Decebalus' invasion, but with the arrival of substantial reinforcements sent by Trajan their situation improved. The Dacians and Roxolani then made the fatal mistake of separating their forces, which enabled the Romans to react by defeating both armies in detail, obliging Decebalus to abandon his plans for the opening of a second front. Trajan then resumed his offensive in Dacia, having reorganized his army on three separate columns. These were to attack the Dacian fortifications from three different directions, each having as their final objective the conquest of Decebalus' capital. The Romans, albeit with great difficulties, were able to secure several Dacian fortifications and started to encircle Sarmizegetusa. At this point, probably in order to gain time and reorganize his defences, Decebalus sent emissaries to Trajan with offers of peace. The Romans responded by proposing very harsh conditions, which could not be accepted by Decebalus. Consequently, military operations soon resumed and during the following weeks the Romans besieged and captured all the Dacian fortifications located around Sarmizegetusa. The Dacians attacked the Roman troops while they were besieging the last stronghold, but their offensive was repulsed with heavy losses. The way to the Dacian capital was now open for the Romans – Decebalus' army had been defeated on the open field and there were no fortifications left in Dacian hands. The Romans, however, were extremely tired: they had suffered significant losses since the beginning of the war and were by now very far from their own provinces. The siege of Sarmizegetusa would have lasted for months, the city being heavily fortified and built on top of a mountain, and Trajan could not sustain a new campaign in a hostile land, especially without proper supplies and fresh reinforcements. As a result, he decided to terminate hostilities and to conclude a peace treaty with Decebalus. The conditions imposed by the Romans to the Dacians were very harsh: Decebalus had to accept the presence of several Roman garrisons on his territory and was forced to give up all the weapons of his army. In addition, he was to destroy all the fortifications of his realm and to cede part of his southern territories to the Roman Empire. Finally, the Dacians were required to accept Rome's protection, thereby transforming their kingdom into a client state of the Empire. Decebalus had no choice but to accept these humiliating conditions in order to gain time to prepare for a new war against Rome. In AD 102, military operations finally came to an end, at least for the moment.

Soon after Trajan abandoned the theatre of operations with most of his troops, Decebalus started planning for another conflict with Rome. He re-equipped his whole army with new weapons and rebuilt the fortifications around his capital that had been destroyed by the Romans. He attacked the Iazyges to punish them for their neutrality and ordered the execution of all those Dacian nobles who were in favour of respecting the peace treaty signed with the Romans. In June AD 105, Trajan responded to these events and moved at the head of his forces back towards Moesia. When the Roman army arrived on the Danube, Trajan learned that his garrisons in Dacia had been massacred and that Decebalus was already waiting for him north of the river. Many Roman fortresses of the Danubian *limes* (i.e. border) had been attacked and occupied by the Dacians, so Trajan had to spend the entire summer of that year retaking the positions that had been recently lost. During this early phase of the war, the Romans realized that it had been a mistake not to besiege Sarmizegetusa beforehand: it was clear by now that the only way to secure the Danubian frontier was to defeat Dacia and annex it to the Empire. Decebalus was too intelligent and ambitious to be a vassal king, so it was essential to conclude the new conflict with his capture or execution. Knowing how difficult it would be to conquer the whole of the Dacian Kingdom, Trajan remained south of the Danube until AD 106, using this period to reorganize the defences of Moesia and assemble more troops for the coming invasion. During these crucial months of preparation, the Romans also completed the construction of a permanent bridge across the Danube. Thanks to this, Roman forces were able to move north at any time and to receive supplies and reinforcements much more easily than in the previous conflict. The Dacians were impressed by the building of this bridge, which was an incredible achievement for the time, but could do little to destroy it since it was defended by a substantial number of Roman troops. When it became clear that Trajan would cross the Danube at the head of a massive invasion force, the main allies of Decebalus abandoned the Dacians to their fate. The Roxolani and Bastarnae, who had made up a major portion of Decebalus' armies during the previous conflict, changed their political attitude and proclaimed their neutrality in a bid to avoid the bloody vengeance of the Romans. While these events took place north of the Danube, Trajan worked hard to receive military support from the Iazyges and the Germanic tribes that were settled on Dacia's north-western border. He wanted to be sure that these peoples would not collaborate with Decebalus, and also hoped that they would attack Dacia from other directions in order to open other fronts on his enemy's frontiers. Learning that Decebalus had been abandoned by his allies, the Romans initiated a further invasion of Dacia. The Roman army was divided into two large columns: one would attack the fortifications of Sarmizegetusa from the west – forcing the Iron Gates – while the other attacked from the east.

The Roman advance was very difficult and slow, the Dacian warriors putting up a strong resistance and defending their homeland to the last man. However, the fortifications rebuilt by Decebalus after AD 102 proved to be of inferior quality

Germanic warrior of the Bastarnae, armed with throwing javelins. (*Photo and copyright by Ancient Thrace*)

Dacian warlord. (*Photo and copyright by Historia Renascita*)

compared to those that had been constructed several years before with the assistance of Roman military engineers. As a result, they were all overcome by the advancing Romans and their garrisons were either killed or captured. By the end of summer of AD 106, all the Dacian fortified positions around Sarmizegetusa had been taken and the two Roman columns could join forces. Trajan was now ready to besiege the Dacian capital with his superior forces, but had to act swiftly as winter was coming and it would have been impossible for his troops to conduct a long siege on high ground in cold temperatures. Trajan was determined not to make the same mistake again: Sarmizegetusa had to be taken and Decebalus had to be neutralized, at all costs. The siege, against all expectations, did not last long: the fighting between the besieged and the besiegers was brutal, but the Dacians had lost most of their best warriors during previous combats and their population was exhausted. When the Roman soldiers entered the city, many Dacian leaders – realizing all was lost – committed suicide in order to avoid capture. Yet Decebalus did not consider the fall of his capital to be a mortal blow, and he abandoned Sarmizegetusa before the end of the siege and fled north. The Dacian king knew the territory of his realm very well and had a clear idea how he could continue resisting the Roman invaders. He moved to the densely forested areas of the Carpathians, where he aimed to raise another army and start planning a new campaign, one that would be conducted with guerrilla methods since the Romans were by now too numerous to be faced in a pitched battle.

The northern part of Dacia was the wildest of Decebalus' kingdom, located far from the Danube and being crossed by few roads. The Dacians could potentially have held out for years in the Carpathians, Decebalus hoping that a long resistance would give him enough time to form new alliances with the Sarmatians and to raise more warriors. Meanwhile, Trajan, after seizing Sarmizegetusa, formed a special column of elite Roman troops and sent it to the north with orders to capture or kill Decebalus. Although the Dacian king was no longer a menace to the stability of the Empire, since he commanded only a few retainers, if not neutralized he could have resumed control of his kingdom by organizing a revolt of the Dacians against the Romans. The troops sent into northern Dacia had great difficulties in tracking down the enemy and had to advance very slowly through unknown lands in which the terrain was perfect for ambushes. The Dacians obtained some minor successes in this phase of the conflict, usually by attacking small Roman parties with hit-and-run tactics. Despite this, time was running out for Decebalus, who had been unable to conclude an alliance with the Sarmatians. His military resources remained quite limited and the Romans were gradually conquering northern Dacia. Eventually, during one of the many skirmishes that took place in this final part of the war, Decebalus and his retainers were intercepted by an auxiliary Roman cavalry unit. Surrounded by enemy

Dacian heavy cavalryman with *draco* standard. (*Photo and copyright by Historia Renascita*)

Dacian chieftain playing a war horn. (*Photo and copyright by Historia Renascita*)

soldiers, the great Dacian king decided to commit suicide in order to avoid capture. All the other leaders who were with him did the same, and only a handful of men were captured by the Romans. The head of Decebalus was brought to Trajan a few days later. With the death of the Dacian king, the war finally came to an end. The Romans continued to fight in Dacia for several more months, but only to put down minor revolts that erupted on a local basis. By the end of AD 106, the former Dacian Kingdom had been transformed into a Roman province, comprising a large portion of territory north of the Danube. The fall of the Dacian Kingdom, however, did not mark the end of the Dacians as an independent people. Many of them abandoned their homeland after the Roman conquest and moved north in search of new lands where they could live according to their traditions. These became known as Free Dacians, in order to distinguish them from the majority of the Dacians who remained in their homeland under Roman rule.

# Chapter 8

# The Decline of the Sarmatians

The Free Dacians settled on territories that were already inhabited by peoples of Dacian stock and by many Sarmatians. These areas are today part of south-western Ukraine, Moldavia and Bessarabia (a region of Romania). The two main communities of Dacian stock there were the Costoboci and the Carpi. The Costoboci lived between the Carpathians and the Dniestr River, while the Carpi were between the Siret River and the Prut River. From an ethnic point of view, they were part of the Dacians, but they had never been included in the Dacian Kingdom. Across the decades they had been strongly influenced by the material culture of the Sarmatians, and thus were quite different from the ordinary Dacians. The Costoboci and the Carpi soon absorbed the refugees from the Dacian Kingdom inside their own communities, becoming part of the Free Dacians. They then started to launch frequent raids against Roman Dacia, apparently never accepting the loss of their homeland and always hoping that the Romans would abandon it. Their hopes were buoyed by the fact that the northern borders of Dacia were particularly difficult to defend for the Romans, as there was no great river like the Danube to use as a natural barrier and the frontier was too long to be defended with the construction of a wall. The incursions of the Free Dacians started around AD 120, but were not perceived as a great danger by the Romans, because they were restricted to rapid raids conducted by limited numbers of warriors. Over time, however, the Roman defences along the northern frontier came under increasing pressure. Germanic tribes initiated their migrations towards the Empire and attacked the western Danubian *limes*, prompting large parts of the Roman army to be deployed in that sector of the northern border, meaning the military presence in Dacia was much reduced. The Dacians and their Sarmatian allies took advantage of this changing situation and attacked Roman Dacia several times between AD 120 and 275. As time progressed, they did not limit themselves to quick raids, but organized proper invasions of their ancient homeland. Several emperors had to fight against the Free Dacians for more than two centuries: Antoninus Pius in AD 157, Maximinus I in AD 238, Decius in AD 250, Gallienus in AD 257, Aurelian in AD 272 and Constantine the Great in AD 337. Until AD 275, the Romans were forced to garrison Dacia with large forces in order to contain the incursions of the Free Dacians. There were always at least two legions and forty

Dacian heavy infantryman. (*Photo and copyright by Historia Renascita*)

auxiliary corps in the province, a total of around 35,000 soldiers. On many occasions, these were barely sufficient to save Dacia from devastating raids. In AD 275, Emperor Aurelian decided to evacuate Dacia, considering it impossible to defend. At that time, the Roman Empire was under attack along all its borders and there were insufficient resources to face all the threats. Dacia was greatly exposed to foreign attacks and needed too many troops to be defended effectively, so the Romans abandoned the province and moved south of the Danube, where they established their new

Dacian heavy infantryman. (*Photo and copyright by Historia Renascita*)

*limes*. All the Roman inhabitants of Dacia migrated to Moesia, meaning the local population could regain its independence. After centuries of battles and hardships, the Free Dacians had finally achieved their objective. In AD 337, Constantine the Great briefly reoccupied part of Dacia, but his successors were obliged to evacuate it again – this time forever. Unfortunately for the Dacians, their new-found freedom did not last long, as a few years later they were wiped out by the Goths who invaded Eastern Europe.

During the period from AD 120–180, before the incursions of the Free Dacians into Roman Dacia became significant, the Romans had to face deadly attacks from the Sarmatians and their new Germanic allies, the Marcomanni. These were some of the bloodiest conflicts ever fought by the Roman Empire, and according to several scholars marked the beginning of Rome's military decline. The *Bellum Germanicum and Sarmaticum* (German and Sarmatian War) included several defeats for the Romans, who had to employ all their resources in order to stop the migrations of the Germanic tribes on the Danubian frontier. Since the last phase of Augustus' reign, the Romans had understood that conquering Germany was an impossible task for them and that they had to adopt a defensive attitude in the border regions of their dominions. This worked well until the age of Trajan, when the Empire reached its maximum territorial expansion and the Germanic tribes were easily contained by the *limes* and the Roman forces garrisoning it. When Marcus Aurelius became emperor, however, the situation started to change very rapidly, the Roman Empire being shattered by the outbreak of a terrible epidemic known as the Antonine Plague that arrived in Europe from the Parthian territories of the Middle East (it was probably transported by the legionaries serving in Mesopotamia). The plague killed around 7 million people and seriously damaged the economy of the Empire. While these events took place in Roman lands, the Great Migrations of the Germanic tribes started in Central Europe. The Goths began moving from their homeland at the mouth of the River Vistula, being under strong pressure from the steppe peoples of Central Asia. This migration of the Goths forced the Germanic tribes living on the borders of the Roman Empire – which had been quiet until then – to start moving west towards the Rhine and south towards the Danube. The first Germanic incursions across the *limes*, during AD 162–165, were easily repulsed by the Romans, but these were just the beginning of a much bigger process. This became apparent when the Germanic Vandals and Sarmatian Iazyges invaded Dacia, killing its governor and devastating its territory. Meanwhile, the Marcomanni crossed the Danube and attacked the Roman province of Pannonia (present-day Hungary) from the north. Marcus Aurelius initially decided to concentrate his efforts in Dacia against the Sarmatians, realizing that the province was particularly exposed to foreign invasions. In the west, however, the situation became particularly serious when the Marcomanni and their warlord Ballomar established a confederation of tribes with the clear intention of conquering Pannonia. In AD 170, at the bloody Battle of Carnutum, 20,000 Roman soldiers were defeated by Ballomar's warriors, after which the Romans were expelled from Pannonia and the Germanic invaders continued their advance towards Noricum (present-day Austria) and northern Italy. This was the first time that foreign invaders attacked the Italian peninsula since 101 BC, when the Cimbri and Teutones had raided north-western Italy.

After these events, which had a great symbolic impact on Rome, Marcus Aurelius decided to concentrate all his military strength against the Marcomanni in Italy. By the end of AD 171, the Germanic warriors had been expelled from northern Italy and Marcus Aurelius was ready to launch a punitive expedition north of the Danube. The ensuing Germanic campaign of AD 172 was a success for Rome, but it did not destroy the great military potential of the Marcomanni. In AD 173 and 174, the Romans obtained a decisive victory over the Quadi, another Germanic tribe that was the main ally of the Marcomanni, after which they could focus on defending Dacia and Moesia from the Iazyges (who had not yet been defeated). A new *Expeditio Sarmatica* (Sarmatian Expedition) was organized, which ended in AD 175 with a great victory for the Romans. The Sarmatians were forced to return all the Romans they had captured in the previous campaigns – some 100,000 people in total – and were obliged to provide 8,000 mounted auxiliaries to the Roman army. These cavalrymen, equipped in the traditional Sarmatian way, were sent to Britannia by the Roman authorities and remained there to protect the northern borders from the incursions of the Celtic tribes settled in Scotland. During the military events described above, the Free Dacians always sided with the Iazyges and participated in all the incursions directed against the Roman province of Dacia. By AD 175, both the Sarmatians and the Marcomanni had been temporarily defeated by the Romans and it seemed that Marcus Aurelius was on the verge of annexing their territories to the Empire. Indeed, there were plans to create two new provinces, Marcomannia and Sarmatia. However, an internal rebellion prevented the emperor from securing possession of the new lands that had been occupied north of the Danube. In AD 177, the Marcomanni and the Quadi rose up in revolt against Rome, having never truly accepted becoming clients of the Empire. The Quadi were crushed after a terrible campaign that was conducted on the territory of present-day Slovakia, and by AD 180 they no longer represented a threat to Rome. In that same year, however, Marcus Aurelius died, which proved a terrible blow for the Roman army as his successor, Commodus, did not have the same strategic vision as his father and possessed little interest in military matters. Without proper leadership, the Roman forces were unable to effectively defend the frontiers.

Commodus hastily concluded a peace treaty with the Marcomanni that did nothing to resolve the problems of the northern *limes*. Meanwhile, the Free Dacians and the Sarmatians also rebelled against the Empire and resumed their attacks against Dacia. In AD 182, Rome was able to obtain a victory in that sector of the Danubian frontier, but it was not a decisive success. After Marcus Aurelius' death, the border regions of the Roman Empire never experienced a long period of peace. The Marcomannic Wars had shown the military weakness of the Empire, which was no longer able to protect the long *limes*. The Marcomanni and the Quadi were soon joined by other Germanic tribes from the eastern regions of Europe, and these, exerting strong pressure on Roman territories, eventually caused the fall of the Empire.

Following the end of the Dacian Wars, the Roxolani and the Iazyges fought a number of wars against each other and became increasingly weak militarily. Between AD 236 and 305, the Iazyges launched a series of incursions against Roman provinces in the Balkans, obtaining some minor successes, but on several occasions they were defeated by the emperors facing them. After the Goths began migrating across Eastern Europe, thousands of Sarmatians were allowed by the Romans to settle on the territories of the Empire as *foederati* (allies). The Romans appreciated the quality of the Sarmatian heavy cavalry and always tried to include large numbers of Sarmatian horsemen in their armies. By settling Sarmatian tribes on the frontier areas of the Empire, the Romans could count on some excellent military contingents tasked with defending the imperial borders from Germanic incursions. Many Sarmatian aristocrats obtained Roman citizenship and several Sarmatian colonies were created across the Roman Empire, including some far from the frontier areas. The ascendancy of the Goths in Eastern Europe had extremely negative consequences for the Sarmatians, who were defeated on several occasions by the migrating Germanic warriors. The Sarmatian tribes also came under attack from another people of the steppes: the Alans. These probably originated from the fusion of some eastern Sarmatian and Massagetae groups. The Alans, after entering the Pontic Steppe, soon became the dominant military power there, replacing the Sarmatians exactly like they had done with the Scythians. Pressed by the superior numbers of the Goths and the Alans, the Sarmatians had no choice but to migrate inside the Roman Empire. A large number of Sarmatian warriors enlisted in the Roman army, while most of the Sarmatian civilians sought refuge in Thrace and Macedonia. By AD 400, the Sarmatians had mostly been absorbed by the Roman Empire, except for a few communities that became part of the Alans. With the ascendancy of the Huns in the early years of the fifth century AD, both the Alans and the Goths lost their prominence in the Pontic Steppe and became – albeit temporarily – vassals of the Hunnic Empire. When the power of the Huns crumbled following Attila's death in AD 453, the Alans moved to

Dacian archer. (*Photo and copyright by Historia Renascita*)

Display of Dacian helmets. (*Photo and copyright by Historia Renascita*)

the northern part of the Caucasus and the Goths resumed their migration towards the Rhine. As for the Bosporan Kingdom, around AD 250 it came under attack from the Goths, but despite being greatly weakened it continued to survive as an autonomous political entity until it was finally overrun by the Huns around AD 375.

# Chapter 9

# Military Organization and Equipment of the Sarmatians

Differently from those of the Scythian, Sarmatian armies consisted almost entirely of cavalry because none of the Sarmatian tribes were ever fully 'hellenized' like some of the Scythians. Like for all the peoples of the steppes, each able-bodied Sarmatian male was a warrior and capable of fighting under the guidance of his tribal leader. As with the Scythians, the poorest Sarmatians served as horse archers, whereas the richest ones made up a military caste of professional warriors who were equipped as heavy cavalry and made up the personal retinues of the various noble warlords. The professional warriors belonging to the same retinue were linked by strong personal bonds, swearing oaths of friendship and loyalty to each other which were sealed during special ceremonies by drinking drops of each other's blood mixed with wine. The early Sarmatian armies, like the Scythian ones, included a majority of horse archers acting as auxiliaries for an elite minority of heavily armoured cavalry, so their battlefield tactics were exactly the same as those employed by the Scythians. As time progressed, however, an important evolutionary process took place within the Sarmatian mounted forces. Frequently facing the Roman legions, they started to modify their balance between horse archers and heavy cavalry. Combat experience showed how mounted archers had great difficulty in defeating a Roman heavy infantry force. The Sarmatian heavy cavalrymen, however, often achieved clear victories over the Roman legionaries thanks to the deadly impact of their frontal charges. Consequently, the number of horse archers in the Sarmatian armies decreased considerably, while the importance of the heavy contingents consisting of professional fighters increased massively. The Sarmatians are lauded as having invented a new form of super-heavy cavalry known by the Greeks as cataphracts (a term meaning 'covered with armour'). Basically, a cataphract was a horseman covered with full armour who rode a fully armoured horse and was equipped with the *kontus* heavy lance. He was capable of crushing any heavy infantry formation deployed by the enemy. According to ancient sources, the new troop type of armoured lancers was invented by the Sarmatians, but in reality they merely imported them to Europe from the Asian regions of Bactria and Sogdia, where cataphracts had originated from the Saka during the fifth century BC. When the Sarmatians faced the Scythians on the open field for the first, at the Battle of the River Thatis, their cavalry still consisted of lightly equipped horse archers, cataphracts only becoming a significant component of the Sarmatian armies during the first century AD. The adoption of the *kontus* as the new main weapon of the Sarmatian heavy cavalry was probably the result of the defeats they suffered at the hands of the Hellenistic phalangites from the Kingdom of Pontus. The great Roman historian Tacitus was the first ancient writer to describe in full detail the distinctive panoply of the Sarmatian cataphracts. Despite wearing super-heavy equipment, the cataphracts were extremely flexible tactically and could perform effective feigned retreats. Like the Scythians, the Sarmatians also had lightly armed infantry contingents provided by the local communities of Ukraine and southern Russia that had been submitted by them. These, however, only performed auxiliary military duties of little importance.

The early Sarmatian heavy cavalry was mostly equipped with corselets made of leather, covered with scales of the same material. Over time, however, corselets with bronze or iron scales almost identical to those worn by the Scythians came into standard use. Noble and professional warriors wore corselets entirely covered with metal scales, while common fighters usually only had some bronze or iron plates applied on key points of their leather corselets. When covered with scales, corselets usually reached the mid-thigh and had a slit at each side extending up to the waistbelt in order to facilitate riding. A leather belt secured the cuirass high

Display of Dacian swords. (*Photo and copyright by Historia Renascita*)

around the waist, taking much of its weight off the shoulders. According to the most recent findings, Sarmatian corselets mainly had iron scales because bronze became less popular during the first century AD. By the time of the Dacian Wars, several Sarmatian heavy horsemen started to replace their scale armour with chainmail cuirasses, but these were quite difficult and costly to produce. As an alternative, the poorest warriors could wear leather corselets covered with scales made from horn or horse-hooves. According to ancient sources, the Sarmatians experienced serious difficulties in finding enough iron for producing their military equipment after the Romans conquered Dacia, and had to start using alternative materials for the scales of their cuirasses. During the early decades of their presence in the Pontic Steppe, the Sarmatians wore Greek-style helmets mostly produced in the cities of the Bosporan Kingdom. These – of the Corinthian, Chalcidian and Attic models – were sometimes modified by the Sarmatians by cutting away their lower parts to improve vision for the wearer. The Sarmatians also wore Celtic Montefortino helmets, which they bought or copied from the Bastarnae living in the northern Balkans. A new kind of helmet gradually replaced all the previous models used by the Sarmatians: the spangenhelm. This term is clearly of Germanic origin, with 'spangen' referring to the metal strips that formed the framework of the helmet while 'helm' simply means helmet. The characteristic metal strips of a spangenhelm connected between three and six steel or bronze plates to create a framework of a conical design, which curved with the shape of the head and culminated in a point. The front of the helmet generally included a nasal. Spangenhelms could also incorporate chainmail as neck protection, forming a sort of aventail on the back. Some surviving examples also include eye protection, with a shape that resembles modern eyeglass frames, while others have a full face mask. Older spangenhelms often had cheek flaps made from metal or leather. In general, the spangenhelm offered effective protection for the head and was relatively easy and cheap to produce. The defensive equipment of the Sarmatian heavy cavalrymen was completed by the shield, which was made of wood covered with metal scales, exactly like the standard shield employed by most of the Scythian warriors. Once the Sarmatian heavy cavalry were re-equipped as cataphracts and adopted the *kontus* as their main offensive weapon, shields ceased to be used by them. Nevertheless, light cavalry and the small infantry contingent continued to carry simple wicker shields until the Sarmatians disappeared from history. The Sarmatian heavy cavalry *kontus* was held two-handed: the left arm aiming and supporting the weapon's weight while the right arm thrust from the hip.

The main offensive weapon of the Sarmatian mounted archers was the composite bow, which had all the same features already described for the Scythian composite bow. From the fourth century BC onwards, this was improved by the addition of bone

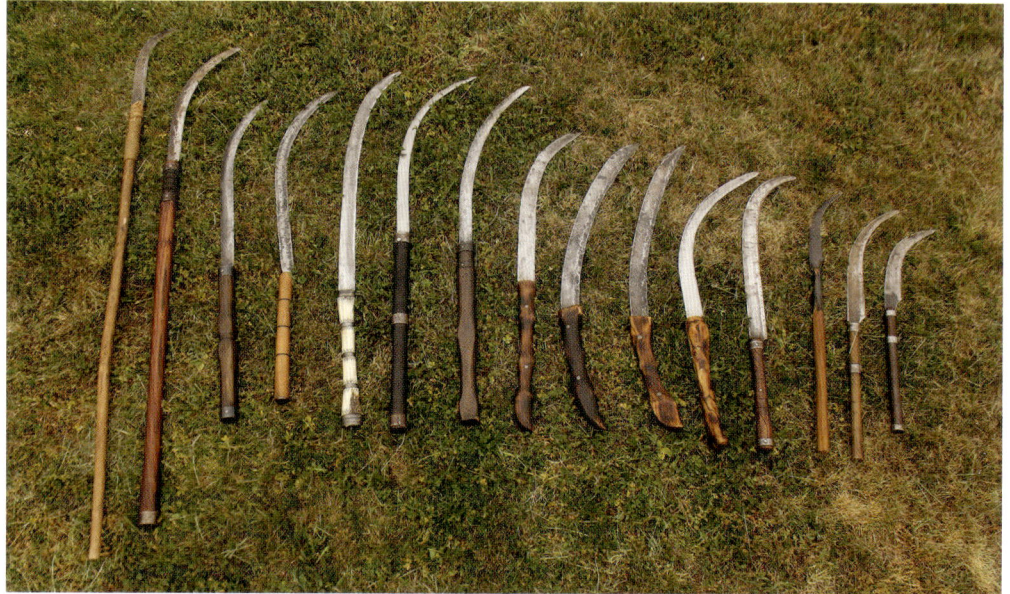

Various models of Dacian weapons derived from the sickle. (*Photo and copyright by Historia Renascita*)

laths at the grip and 'ears' (ends), which gave additional power to the weapon. The Sarmatians also employed the same type of *gorytos* case as the Scythians. During the first century AD, the Sarmatians began using a new model of composite bow, which was probably designed by the Hunnic tribes and thus was known as a Hunnish bow. This measured 120cm in length, which made it much more powerful than the Scythian bow. Indeed, it was probably the adoption of this new weapon that determined the victory of the Sarmatians in the battles fought on the Pontic Steppe against the Scythians. The Hunnish bow was usually asymmetrical in shape, with the top 'half' above the grip being longer. It was too big to be carried in the traditional *gorytos*, so the Sarmatians had to design a new soft bowcase for it. Arrows were carried in two tall cylindrical quivers, which were made of deerskin leather.

The early Sarmatians had long swords very similar to those carried by the Scythians, but with antennae-shaped pommel in the Celtic fashion. These were progressively replaced by new swords with ring-shaped pommels that could be produced in a long version (70–130cm) or a shorter one (60–70cm). The short swords were carried in scabbards secured via two pairs of wings by leather straps that passed around the right thigh, whereas long swords were carried on the left side in conventional scabbards. Sarmatian warriors often had both a long sword for cavalry fighting and a short sword for hand-to-hand combat. Like most nomadic peoples of the steppes, the Scythians and Sarmatians were experts in the use of the lasso, which was employed while moving cattle from one place to another but could also become a weapon. The

Sarmatians, according to ancient sources, were capable of tossing the lasso over an enemy's neck to pull him from his horse.

The horse armour employed by the Sarmatian cataphracts consisted of full cuirasses covered with leather or iron scales. Sarmatian saddles, differently from Scythian ones, had four horns at their angles, which gave much greater stability to an armoured lancer while charging. The Sarmatians were the inventors of the famous *draco* standard, which was later adopted by Roman cavalry. As its name suggests, this had the form of a dragon, with open wolf-like jaws containing several metal tongues. The hollow head of the dragon was made of metal and was mounted on a pole, and it had a long fabric tube fixed to the rear. When in use, the *draco* was held up high so that it filled with air and made a shrill sound as the wind passed through its metal tongues. It was an effective weapon of psychological warfare, especially during the early phases of a pitched battle. The *draco* standard also had another important function in steppe warfare, providing wind-direction for the archers in battle.

# Bibliography

**Primary sources**
Appian, *Roman History*.
Arrian, *Anabasis of Alexander*.
Diodorus Siculus, *History*.
Dionysios of Halikarnassos, *Roman Antiquities*.
Herodotus, *The Histories*.
Livy, *History of Rome from its Foundation*.
Plutarch, *Lives*.
Polybius, *The Histories*.
Strabo, *Geography*.
Thucydides, *History of the Peloponnesian War*.
Xenophon, *Anabasis*.

**Secondary sources**
Anderson, E.B., *Cataphracts: Knights of the Ancient Eastern Empires* (Pen & Sword, 2016).
Baker, P., *Armies and Enemies of Imperial Rome* (Wargames Research Group, 1981).
Brzezinski, R. and Mielczarek, M., *The Sarmatians 600 BC–AD 450* (Osprey Publishing, 2002).
Cernenko, E.V., *The Scythians 700–300 BC* (Osprey Publishing, 1983).
Connolly, P., *Greece and Rome at War* (Frontline Books, 2011).
Dean, S.E., 'Cataphracts: Heavy Cavalry of the Mithridatic Wars', *Ancient Warfare Magazine*, volume X, issue 3.
Everson, T., *Warfare in Ancient Greece: Arms and Armour from the Heroes of Homer to Alexander the Great* (The History Press, 2005).
Goldsworthy, A., *The Fall of the West: The Slow Death of the Roman Superpower* (Weidenfeld & Nicolson, 2009).
Gorelik, K., *Warriors of Eurasia* (Montvert Publishing, 1995).
Head, D., *Armies of the Macedonian and Punic Wars* (Wargames Research Group, 1982).
Head, D., *The Achaemenid Persian Army* (Montvert Publications, 1992).
Karasulas, A., *Mounted Archers of the Steppe 600 BC–AD 1300* (Osprey Publishing, 2004).
Nikonorov, V.P., *The Armies of Bactria 700 BC–AD 450* (Montvert Publications, 1997).
Quesada Sanz, F., *Armas de Grecia y Roma* (La Esfera, 2014).
Sekunda, N., *The Ancient Greeks* (Osprey Publishing, 1986).
Sekunda, N., *The Army of Alexander the Great* (Osprey Publishing, 1984).
Warry, J., *Warfare in the Classical World* (Salamander Books, 1997).
Webber, C., *The Thracians 700 BC–AD 46* (Osprey Publishing, 2001).
Wilcox, P. and Embleton, G., *Rome's Enemies 1: Germanics and Dacians* (Osprey Publishing, 1982).

# The Re-enactors who Contributed to this Book

**Amages Drachen**
Amages Drachen is a re-enactment group created by means of living history, through reconstructions of clothing and artefacts to make history tangible. Our members come from the Rhine-Main area and are committed to teaching and depicting ancient steppe cultures. Both Scythian and Sarmatian representations from the period of about 600 BC up to *circa* AD 300, which we have produced on the basis of archaeological finds and historical sources, are part of our repertoire. We would like to introduce event visitors to the material culture of ancient steppe nomads with self-made replicas, explanations and lectures. The steppe belt today includes large parts of Ukraine, Russia, Kazakhstan, Kyrgyzstan and Mongolia, and was inhabited in ancient times by nomadic tribes, in particular the Scythians, Saka, Sauromatians and Sarmatians, who are also part of our representations. Unfortunately, these nomadic cultures have left no written record of themselves. Knowledge about these scripture-free cultures can today only be obtained from archaeological finds and written sources of neighbouring cultures. From the first millennium BC until late Antiquity, these ancient nomads were in constant contact with the settled high cultures on the edge of the steppe belt: Persians, Chinese, Greeks and Romans. These cultural contacts were both peaceful and warlike: the nomads benefited from the trade routes through the steppe areas (the Silk Road), but the mounted archers were also dreaded warriors and coveted mercenaries. Despite this, these 'milk-drinkers' and 'horse-bowers', as they were called by ancient authors, are rarely found in current written history, but they have always had a decisive influence on European history and have contributed to shape the present-day face of Europe.

*Contacts:*
E-mail: amages.drachen@gmx.de
Website: https://www.sarmaten-steppenkultur.de/index.php/en/home-3/

**Ancient Thrace**
Ancient Thrace living history association was created as a historical re-enactment group in 2015 by enthusiasts from Yambol in Bulgaria, who were fascinated by

the ancient history of their land and wanted to express their passion for it. The group now has around twenty permanent members, along with many friends from different places who often join its activities. The group's main aim is to reconstruct the lifestyle, culture and military equipment of the Thracian tribes in the period from 400 BC–AD 100. With the progression of time, we also started to reconstruct other peoples living in the Balkans during Antiquity: Celts (300 BC–AD 100), Germani (AD 100–200) and Goths (AD 300–400). In our activities and reconstructions we try to be as historically accurate as we can. Our equipment is based on countless hours of interpreting ancient documents and archaeological evidence, and our process of research and experimentation never stops. During recent years we have participated in several festivals in Bulgaria and further afield, and have also collaborated in the creation of movies and books. All these positive experiences have increased our confidence and stimulated the general improvement of our group. Since we created Ancient Thrace, we have visited amazing destinations and met many great people, learned more about history and shared good memories together. For us, historical re-enactment is a special passion that combines our interest in history with our desire to learn more about the past. We wish to reach people and share with them the emotions of this passion, which has become a very important component of our daily life.

*Contacts:*
Facebook: https://www.facebook.com/AncientThrace/

## Historia Renascita

Historia Renascita is a re-enactment association from Romania which creates historical reconstructions of three different periods of Romanian history: the era of the Dacian civilization, from the reign of Burebista until the end of the Daco-Roman Wars (200 BC–AD 200), with special attention to the conquest of Decebalus' Dacian Kingdom by the Romans of Emperor Trajan in AD 106; the period of the Kievan Rus (Middle Ages); and the Great War. Regarding the ancient period, Historia Renascita reconstructs Dacian warriors and civilians, Roman legionaries (of the *Legio IV Flavia Felix*) and other peoples from the *Barbaricum* with which the Dacians came into contact (Celts, Sarmatians and Germani). Historia Renascita had gained great experience in reconstructing the daily life of ancient peoples by participating during the last five years in more than seventy major festivals in Romania and other European countries. Our approach to historical re-enactment is a professional one, based on a rich documentation that is made up of historical and archaeological sources. We create our activities and reconstructions with the help of specialists and researchers whose competences are centred on the history of ancient Dacia. Our activities in experimental archaeology try to be as accurate as possible and are all based on material discoveries or on written accounts provided by ancient historians (such as Strabo, Dio Cassius, Trogus Pompeius, Iordanes, Plutarch, Ovid and many others). Obviously, we also analyze the iconography of important ancient monuments such as Trajan's Column, the Tropaeum Traiani and the Dacian statues from the former Forum of Trajan (some of which adorned Constantine's Arch of Triumph in Rome). We also consult all the latest academic studies and essays published on the history of ancient Dacia. The main objective of Historia Renascita is to provide a significant contribution to the divulging of history, by trying to present all relevant aspects in a balanced and objective way. The photographs reproduced in this book reconstruct accurately all the main typologies of Dacian warriors and were created with the help of photographers from the Alpha Studio of Pitesti in Romania, whom we thank for their precious support.

*Contacts:*
Email: historia.renascita@gmail.com
Facebook: https://www.facebook.com/historiarenascita/

# Index

Amyntas, 49–50
Aristagoras, 36, 39
Attila, 138

Bartatua, 8–9

Croesus, 24

Diophantes, 80, 105

Eumelus, 75

Golden Fleece, 23
Gyges, 6, 8

Harpagus, 24
Herodotus, 1, 4, 23, 29, 90
Homer, 4, 16

Jason, 23

Kimmerikon, 21

Madyes, 8–9
Myrmekion, 21

Nymphaion, 22

Oxyartes, 65, 68, 70

Satyrus, 74–5
Scorilo, 116
Sertorius, 83, 86
Sitalces, 45–6
Spartocus, 19
Strabo, 23, 105

Theodosia, 21
Tyritake, 21

Urartu, 5

*Wanax*, 16

Zopyrion, 71